Praise for
GRACE AFTER MIDNIGHT

"Remarkable."

—*Entertainment Weekly*

"A must-read . . . an unbelievable story of 'I made it.'"

—*Baltimore Times*

"A powerful, slap-in-the-face kind of book that tells it like it is without candy-coating a thing, but what comes across as the most potent is author and actor Felicia 'Snoop' Pearson's dynamic voice . . . a great, big story you shouldn't miss."

—*Tennessee Tribune*

"Direct and rough . . . as GRACE AFTER MIDNIGHT unfolds, readers will have no choice but to root for Snoop."   —Urbanology

"While Felicia Pearson is a brilliant actor in a truly chilling role, what's most remarkable about 'Snoop' is what she has overcome in her life . . . Snoop's tale goes far deeper than previous books. Snoop defies traditional conventions of gender and sexual preference on the hardest streets in America, and she continues to do so in front of millions of TV viewers."   —*Pathfinders Travel*

"Raw . . . undeniably an entertaining read."   —NewsBlaze.com

"A beacon of light for today's troubled youth . . . a story of curiosity, anger, death, murder, drugs, incarceration, redemption, failure, and love . . . fearless in telling her life story . . . Snoop tells all."

—*Baltimore Afro-American*

"With chilling realism, she portrays an androgynous street assassin, yet her real life story is even more remarkable . . . a tale of horror, violence, and anger. In the end, however, it is a tale of redemption."

—BlackBallot.com

Also by David Ritz

BIOGRAPHY

Divided Soul: The Life of Marvin Gaye
Faith in Time: The Life of Jimmy Scott

AUTOBIOGRAPHY

Brother Ray (with Ray Charles)
Inside My Life (with Smokey Robinson)
The Rhythm and the Blues (with Jerry Wexler)
Rage to Survive (with Etta James)
Blues All Around Me (with B. B. King)
Guide to Life (with Sinbad)
From These Roots (with Aretha Franklin)
The Brothers (with the Neville Brothers)
Reach (with Laila Ali)
Guillaume (with Robert Guillaume)
Howling at the Moon (with Walter Yetnikoff)
Elvis by the Presleys (editor)
Messengers: Portraits of African American Ministers
What I Know for Sure (with Tavis Smiley)
Rickles' Book (with Don Rickles)

NOVELS

Search for Happiness
The Man Who Brought the Dodgers Back to Brooklyn
Dreams
Blue Notes Under a Green Felt Hat
Barbells and Saxophones
Family Blood
Passion Flowers
Sanctified Blues (with Mable John)
Stay Out of the Kitchen (with Mable John)

GRACE AFTER MIDNIGHT

A MEMOIR

FELICIA "SNOOP" PEARSON

AND DAVID RITZ

GRAND CENTRAL
PUBLISHING

NEW YORK   BOSTON

Grand Central Publishing
Hachette Book Group
237 Park Avenue
New York, NY 10017

Visit our website at www.HachetteBookGroup.com.

Printed in the United States of America

Originally published in hardcover by Grand Central Publishing.

First Trade Edition: November 2009
10 9 8 7 6 5 4 3 2 1

Grand Central Publishing is a division of Hachette Book Group, Inc.
The Grand Central Publishing name and logo is a trademark of Hachette Book Group, Inc.

The Library of Congress has cataloged the hardcover edition as follows:

Pearson, Felicia, 1980–
    Grace after midnight : a memoir / Felicia Pearson and David Ritz.—1st ed.
        p. cm.
    ISBN: 978-0-446-19518-8
    1. Pearson, Felicia, 1980–   2. Television actors and actresses—United States—Biography.   I. Ritz, David.   II. Title.
    PN2287.P34A3 2007
    791.4502'8092—dc22
    [B]   2007023465

ISBN 978-0-446-19519-5 (pbk.)

THIS BOOK IS FOR ARNOLD LONLY,
THE MAN I CALL UNCLE
R.I.P.

I'm not making excuses, and I'm not feeling sorry for myself. Don't expect you to feel sorry for me either.

Just want to tell my story while it's fresh.

Just want to make sure other people know my story, especially the kids on the streets and the kids working the corners.

Just want to let them know that you can get over without killing people and selling packs.

I did all that. Fact is, I was still doing it up till a couple of years ago.

Then something happened.

This book is about what happened.

BABY GIRL

I was born in Baltimore twenty-seven years ago, and then I died—twice. I died both times because my mother was filled with drugs and so was I. Crack babies are messed-up babies, and, according to what the doctors were saying, I didn't have a prayer.

But they brought me back from death's door. Someone or something keeps bringing me back from death's door.

I don't understand it, but maybe writing this book will help me see who I was and who I became.

Sometimes I close my eyes, take a deep breath, and imagine myself back then:

A little-bitty baby small enough to fit into the palm of the doctor's hand, no bigger than a puppy or kitten; a baby who has to be fed with an eye dropper 'cause her mouth is too small for the nipple of a bottle; a baby born cross-eyed due to the drugs running through her system.

A baby born to die.

But that same doomed-to-die baby finds a way to live.

How?

Why?

Sure wasn't because of Mama. Mama was Loretta Chase. The woman may have wanted me—I can't know that for sure—but I do know that she couldn't care for me. Later I learned that Mother was the kind of lady that always kept a drug dealer around to fill her needs. She could do that because she had a pretty face, long wavy hair, and a fine figure. Men flocked to her. My daddy ran from her—or she chased him off. I never did get the story.

I didn't get a lot of the stories about my real parents. They're ghost figures in my childhood. I saw them in my dreams when I was a little girl. Sometimes they creep back into my dreams now that I'm a grown woman, but they're always covered in mystery.

The mystery was heavy because as soon as I was born I was put into a foster home owned by two people who had a row house in the toughest neighborhood in East Baltimore. Their names were Cora and Levi Pearson and their place was on East Oliver Street, three doors off the corner of North Montford. That's where I grew up. Oliver and Montford is where it all happened.

When I arrived the Pearsons were already in their early sixties. Sweet folk. They took care of me, but I still wanted my mama. And when I heard that Mama was calling for me, I got happy all over. I wanted to see her.

All little girls wanna see their mothers. All girls need their mothers. The earliest dreams I can remember are dreams of my mother. I'd see her standing there before me, holding out her arms, hugging me tight, putting me to bed and tucking me in.

"You're my precious baby," she'd say.

I'd smile at her, close my eyes, and fall asleep inside my dream.

THE CLOSET

My memories of Mama's visits are like dreams.

During the first two visits we were at the park. I remember clouds and rain, I remember a dark sky, wet grass, and plastic slides in the playground. I remember Mrs. Simms, the white social worker, who held my hand until, from behind a tree, a woman appeared. The woman was beautiful. She ran to me with her arms wide open. I didn't move. I didn't know what to do.

"It's your mother," said Mrs. Simms. "Go to your mother."

I let the woman embrace me. She smelled of cigarettes and perfume. Tears ran down her cheek. I didn't know why she was crying. She held me tight and said words I don't remember. I imagine that she said she loved me. We walked for a while. She, Mrs. Simms, and I went to a candy store where I got a soda and a little bag of M & M's.

"You and your mother look just alike," Mrs. Simms said.

I loved hearing those words because I knew my mother looked like a lady in a magazine.

The rain stopped—I can't remember if this was the first visit or the second—and children were in the park. My mother said something about my pigtails. As a little girl, my hair was done up in little pigtails.

"If you let your hair grow out," she said, "it'll look like mine."

She let me touch her wavy hair.

"Can I bring her to my house? Can I be alone with my daughter?" she asked Mrs. Simms.

Mrs. Simms said, "Maybe. Maybe next time."

Next time came soon. The night before I was too excited to sleep.

What would my mother's house look like? I was sure it'd be pretty because she was pretty. I was sure it'd be big. The house on Oliver Street had three floors and three bedrooms, but I knew my mother's house would be bigger. The house on Oliver Street had all sorts of people living there—grand-children and cousins to Mr. and Mrs. Pearson. But I was my mother's only child. I wouldn't have to share the house with anyone but my mother. Maybe I could live with her forever.

I always hated dresses, but I wore one to visit my mother because I wanted to look pretty. I wanted to look like my mother. My dress, lavender and embroidered with white lace, was brand new. My foster mama had bought it for me to wear to church.

My excitement built as Mrs. Simms drove me to my

mother's. But when we arrived, I was sure she had made a mistake. It wasn't a house at all, but a tiny one-room apartment with a small kitchen, and a couch that opened up into a bed. The room was messy and didn't smell good. This couldn't be where my mom lived. But it was.

When Mrs. Simms left us, my mother sat down on the edge of the bed. Something was wrong. She was crying and shaking. I didn't know why. She didn't hug and kiss me like she had in the park. She didn't even look at me. I just stood there.

Then her mood changed. She got up from the bed and told me to take off my clothes. I didn't understand why. I wouldn't do it.

"Do it!" she cried.

She screamed at me until I did it. I took off all my clothes, dropping them on the floor.

"Now get in there," she ordered, pointing to the closet.

I tried to run but my mother caught me. She pushed me into the closet and locked the door behind me. I began wailing at the top on my lungs.

"Stop crying," she said. "I'll be back."

Then the sound of her leaving the apartment.

The darkness.

The fear of being locked in.

Naked fear.

Baby girl fear.

Pure terror.

I carried on. Kept crying. Kept screaming louder, but no

one heard. Cried so loud and long that I cried myself out. I finally fell to the floor and started kicking. I had to get out. Someone had to hear me.

I don't know how much time passed, but when I heard the voices of Mrs. Simms and my foster father, I screamed my head off. They broke open the door and set me free. I was hysterical.

"Imagine that," I heard Mrs. Simms tell my foster father, "selling her little girl's clothes to buy crack."

I was never allowed to be alone with my mother again.

Sometime in my childhood my mother reappeared at the house on Oliver Street.

Each time the visit was short, and with each visit she looked less beautiful. Her eyes were crazy. Sometimes her dress was dirty and worn. She'd come into the front room and just look at me. She'd try to smile, but the smile wouldn't come. She'd cry and leave.

Her visits became more infrequent. Finally they stopped.

That's when Mrs. Pearson became Mama and Mr. Pearson became Pop.

COLD-BLOODED KILLER

For the first eight years of my life, I was not only teased for being a foster child, I was teased for being cross-eyed. Mama told me I looked fine, and so did Pop, but I knew better. I knew because the kids on the block wouldn't leave me alone. They teased me something fierce. They called me weirdo. Called me ugly. "How many fingers am I holding up?" they'd ask. And they'd laugh and say I was blind as a bat.

At first I didn't fight them. I was too small. Their cruelty hurt my heart, but I didn't know what to do about it. Didn't cry. Didn't lash out. Just held it in and kept to myself. Became a loner.

"You ain't ugly," said a handsome man who came to visit one afternoon. "You as pretty as your mama."

He wasn't talking about Cora Pearson. He was talking about Loretta Chase, the woman who took off my clothes and locked me in the closet.

"This here is Bernard," Pop said to me as we sat in the front room. "This here is your real father."

Unlike light-skinned Loretta, this man was black as midnight. Like Loretta, though, he had his hair in waves. He brought me a little doll I didn't want. I didn't like dolls. As he sat there, I looked into his eyes and saw ice. I felt ice.

"You a good girl?" he said.

I looked down at the floor and didn't say nothing.

"You got all those pigtails," he said.

I still didn't say nothing.

He got up and put his hand on my cheek. His hand was cold.

"Be a good girl," he said.

He left without another word.

Later I heard Mama and Pop talking in the kitchen.

"He's a stick-up man," said Mama.

"Worse than that," added Pop. "Man's a cold-blooded killer."

Didn't take long to learn what that meant.

Killing was part of our neighborhood. Death lived on our block. Death was the business of Collins Funeral Home, just down the street. Seemed liked death rode down Oliver Street more often than the ice cream truck. Death was a regular. Even as a baby girl, death—up close and real as rain—was part of my life.

THE SMURFS

Death is a lot for a kid to contend with.

The Smurfs are the opposite of death. Smurfs never die. Smurfs live forever in a dreamland where I want to be.

First time I learn about Smurfs is over a friend's house. They're on TV.

"Who they?" I ask.

"They the Smurfs."

I fall in love with the Smurfs, so deep in love until Mama buys me Smurf sheets and Smurf pillowcases. I have Smurf pictures on the walls and Smurfs cartoons by my bed. I surround myself with Smurfs.

Man, I even have me some Smurf dreams.

In one dream I wake up and I'm not on Oliver Street no more. I'm in a mushroom house. That's right. A house cut out of a big-ass mushroom. Far as I'm concerned, it's a Smurf World. If you don't like it, you can go Smurf yourself.

Got me four fingers like a Smurf. Got me a little white

hat, puffy feet, and Smurfy eyes. I still got my braids. I'm Braidy Smurf.

Braidy Smurf is meeting Brainy Smurf. Here's Hefty Smurf who's got a tattoo on his arm and can kick plenty ass. Harmony Smurf is hanging with Handy Smurf.

I'm chilling with all the Smurfs. Even Smurfette. Especially Smurfette. She's wearing a dress and high heels. She's flirting with me just like she flirts with the boys. Invites me to her crib. I go in and get comfortable.

I'm sure-enough falling for Smurfette.

But if Smurfette is a girl, what does that make me?

In real life, I wasn't relating to girls. I was relating to boys.

In school, the uniform was skirts. But I was bony and didn't like showing my knees. I wanted to wear baggy jeans like the boys. Soon as I got home I got out of that skirt and put on jeans. Got out of that blouse and put on a boy's shirt.

"Put on that cheerleader skirt," Mama said.

"Don't want to."

"You need to, baby," she insisted. "You're going to make an adorable cheerleader. You're pretty as a picture and you're the best little athlete in that school. I want you to try out."

Loved Mama and wanted to make her happy, so I tried out. Went to the audition where they made you dance like Janet Jackson.

Don't get me wrong. I been in love with Janet my whole life. Loved her when she was Penny on *Good Times* with JJ and them. I watched those reruns till I had 'em memorized. When homegirl hit with "Control," I loved her even more. I love her today.

When "Control" dropped, we were all caught up in the videos. "Nasty," "What Have You Done for Me Lately"— those jams were poppin' everywhere I went. But when I went to the cheerleader audition and saw that they wanted me to do Janet's chair routine from "The Pleasure Principle" video, I said, "Thanks, but no thanks." Janet can do that stuff, but not Fefe.

Fefe was what they were calling me when my eyes were still crossed.

"Fefe's fucked up," said one of the boys who saw how I liked to wear jeans and shoot hoops. "Fefe's a straight-up bull dyke."

I didn't know what that meant, but I beat his little ass anyway.

"Fefe's a tomboy," said someone else.

I could deal with that word because it had "boy" in it.

———

The big change for Fefe came when Mama, bless her heart, paid for the operation to fix my eyes. By then I had taken her name, Pearson, and was officially Felicia Pearson. But it didn't take long for Fefe to turn into Snoop. Happened when I was eight. I'll get to that story in a minute.

KNIGHT RIDER

Mama went to a Holy Roller church where everyone was jumping for Jesus. I could feel it. You had to feel the spirit. The music was fresh, the Holy Ghost on the loose, and the people cool. Those big church ladies were out in the kitchen cooking up collard greens, neck bones, and pig's feet. Jesus was all right with me.

Pop was one of those Jehovah's Witnesses. I liked going to his prayer meetings 'cause there were all kinds of folk up in there—black, white, Latino—who thought my pigtails were cute. They were always dropping change in my purse.

But church went on for too long and got me restless. I was an outside kid. Inside bored me. Outside stimulated me. I loved the streets. Loved to sit on the stairs in front of Mama's house and just watch the world go by. Early on, Mama let me wander. She really had no choice 'cause I'd be wandering anyway. Wander down to the corner store where they sold meats and candies. Wander over to the beauty parlor where the women were deep in their dish. Wander to the liquor store where the old winos spun their stories about back in the day. Wander to Gibson's, the sub shop where they got a little arcade with Pac-Man. No one could beat me at Pac-Man.

Wander across the street to play with Curtis. Like me, Curtis followed *Knight Rider* on TV. I didn't know about *Sesame Street* or *Electric Company*, but I sure knew about *Knight Rider*, the show where the star was KITT, a black customized Pontiac Trans-Am. I wanted KITT because KITT could ride through fire. Nothing could stop KITT and nothing could destroy KITT. I had dreams about being in the world of the Knight Rider like I had dreams about being with the Smurfs. In my Knight Rider dreams, when I was commanding that car, nothing could stop me.

You can imagine how happy I was when I got me a toy version of the Knight Rider car.

"How come you don't play with dolls?" asked Curtis.

"How come *you* don't play with dolls?" I asked him.

"I'm a boy. My people say you a butch."

"What's a butch?" I wanted to know.

"That means you ain't right."

"But I got the right Knight Rider, don't I?" I said, holding the car up to the sun and watching the light bounce off it.

"Let me see that thing."

He grabbed the little car from me and let it fly down the street until it knocked into a light pole so hard that black paint chipped off the right door. That got me seeing red. I lost it. I took a swing at Curtis that caught him upside his head. I nearly took his head off. He came back at me, but I was too strong for me. I kept slamming him.

"You a butch," he kept screaming at me.

I slammed him so hard that people passing by had to break it up.

Curtis never fucked with me again.

Back in the crib, Mama used to scold me when she learned I was fighting. After my eye operation I wore glasses for two years. I broke many a pair due to squabbles. I knew Mama wanted me in dresses and ribbons, but Mama was also wise enough to know that wasn't me. Mama knew to accept people the way they are.

Pop got a kick out of having a tomboy. He was a handyman who ran his own little business. He could fix anything mechanical and he liked teaching me. I'd go up on the roof where he taught me to lay tar. Taught me to fix the pipes. When I got a bike—a red-and-black boy's style with the bar under the seat—Pop taught me to take that sucker apart and put it together again. I'd put an empty juice carton on the spokes of the back tire to make that rat-rat-rat-rat noise. Me and the boys would call 'em our dirt bikes. At age eight, that's how we rolled.

Pop would watch me roll down Oliver on my Huffy and smile.

"Girl," he said, "you got an extra dose of get-up-and-go."

Pop had a good dose himself. He'd get up and go visit girlfriends behind Mama's back. Found this out the hard way:

One day we were in the pawnshop where he picked out a gold necklace. He wrote a little card and put it in a box. Because I was looking at all the pistols behind the counter, Pop didn't think I was noticing him. But I noticed everything.

Get home and get ready for dinner. Dinner's always an event at Mama's 'cause you never know who'll show up at the table. Fact is, you never know at any given moment who's living in the house. Mama's grandchildren are always around, not to mention cousins of all ages.

Tonight's macaroni and cheese. Mama puts a hurting on mac and cheese.

"Hey, Mama," I say. "Pop bought you a beautiful necklace."

Pop looks at me like he wants to kick me in the head.

"That's lovely," she says. "Let me see it, Levi."

Pop starts stuttering. "Not sure—not sure where I put it."

"You put it right in your pocket," I say, running over and digging it out for Mama to see.

"There's a card and everything," Mama says.

When she reads the card, though, her eyes turn red as fire. Just like that, she puts Pop's ass out the house. Poor Pop's in the doghouse for weeks. He finally pleads his way back in, but the beautiful thing about the man is that he's not mad at me.

"Give her a whupping for what she done to you," says a cousin of Pop's, a teenaged boy who likes to get high down in our basement where he lives for free. "Whup her bad."

But Pop ain't giving me no whupping.

Pop is saying, "That's my girl. She just told the truth, that's all she did. You can't go off on no one for telling the truth." And with that he'd pat me on the head and have me go with him down the street to fix someone's washing machine.

KEN AND BARBIE

Sheila was Barbie.

I was Ken. I was five, maybe six years old.

We were playing house.

Sheila had golden brown hair. Her body was developing faster than the other girls'. She already had a little booty.

"You the mommy," I said. "I'm the daddy. I just got home from work. How 'bout a kiss?"

Sheila kissed me on the cheek.

"You make dinner," I said. "I gotta go back to work."

"Where you work?" she asked.

"On the streets," I answered.

"What you do?"

"Woman," I said, acting like Pop, "I do what I need to do. I take care of you, that's what I do."

"Do you love me?" she asked.

"Sure," I said. "Ken loves Barbie and Barbie loves Ken. That's how it go."

"We gonna have babies?"

"You want babies?"

"Three," she said. "Two girls and one boy."

"Okay, we'll have babies."

"You know how to make babies?" Sheila wanted to know.

"Well," I hesitated. I really didn't know, but I said, "We just kinda rub together."

We kept our clothes on and just kinda rubbed together.

"Okay," I said, "you wait awhile and then the babies come."

That was our game, and we played it for months.

Sheila was my first girlfriend. Our song was LL Cool J's "I Need Love."

That song had me falling in love with slow jams. Funny to think of me as a little girl dreaming of being the man of the family.

But that's who I was.

Another girl, this one a little older, would sometimes have me sleep over at her house. She'd call it a pajama party. She also liked to play LL's "I Need Love." She also liked to play house.

When we got into bed, she played like she was asleep, and she let me do sneaky shit to her. But I knew she was awake and loving it. She just didn't want to admit it. That was my first experience being with a girl who liked to pretend she wasn't liking it. As time went on, I learned that she wasn't the only one.

I learned that lots of girls have different sexual feelings. The honest ones will admit to it. They'll even talk about it. Sometimes they like a boy. Sometimes they like a girl. Sometimes they like a girl who acts like a boy. I never had problems talking about those different feelings. I did what felt good and natural. Never had no guilt. Never felt like I was doing nothing wrong.

But I'd soon learn that not everyone has an easy attitude about sex. Sex gets people confused, guilty, and crazy. If you're open about your feelings, and those feelings are different from everyone else's, you might be laughed at or even beaten down. You might be secure about your sex life, but the more secure you are, the more insecure you'll make others—especially folks who hate the different sex feelings running through their heads and heating up their hearts.

———

They say your life is secure long as you got a roof over your head.

When I was eight, the roof blew off our house—just like that—and water started flooding in. We ran down to the basement. I thought we'd drown, but we made it through. In 1988, some kind of crazy storm hit Baltimore real hard and nearly did us in.

Next day, though, Pop was up there banging on a new roof.

"Anyone wanna help?" he asked everyone. Mama had some relatives living there that I didn't even know.

No one wanted to help—except me.

"She'll fall off," said a woman I called my aunt.

I paid her no mind, climbed up there and started hammering.

From the streets, a guy looked up and saw me.

"Hey, Levi," he yelled at Pop, "ain't that child labor?"

"This child," Pop yelled back down, "ain't no child. She's smart as a whip and twice as strong as any two boys on this block."

"Well, you keep her close to you, Levi, 'cause this block's getting worse every day. This here is the Wild West."

Pop knew the neighborhood well as anyone. He saw the dangers. He saw how the shit was turning worse before his very eyes. He'd tell me that back in the day it was a nice place to live and raise kids. He'd complain about the hoodlums.

Once I even saw Pop come face to face with a knuckle-head trying to jack him up.

It was the end of the workday. I happened to look out a window and saw Pop walking down the street. That's when a gangsta jumped up outta nowhere and stuck a gun in Pop's back. Pop wheeled around and gave this boy such a heavy look—I mean fire was coming out Pop's eyes—the thug backed down. The gangsta melted into a punk. Never saw nothing like that before. But that was Pops.

He was strong. He worked hard, earned his money, provided for his family. Him and Mama both did things right. They were the right models for a young girl growing up.

So why didn't I grow up the way they wanted me to?

Why couldn't I follow their lead?

Why did I wind up doing the things I did?

The streets were screaming at me—that's for sure. But the streets were screaming at everyone. Some kids ignored those screams. I didn't. I had to see what the screaming was all about.

EVERYTHING MOVES OFF MONEY

If you studied the streets like me, the truth was up in your face: Money made it happen. Money made people jump, duck, hustle, and hide. Big money made *you* big. The lack of money made you little. Your money could be dirty or clean. Didn't matter. Your money could be soaked in fresh blood. That didn't matter either. What mattered was having it. What mattered was getting it. What mattered was keeping it.

To an eight- or nine-year-old child looking at life from the steps of East Oliver Street, it was crystal clear that everything moves off money.

Then when the boys from New York started opening up shop, it became even clearer. New money was taking over.

A shop is where a dealer sets up operation, gets him a couple of corner boys to organize the merchandise and look out for cops, plus a couple of runners who deal with the customers in the cars or the customers walking by.

If you're a kid with half a brain, you scope out the scene in no time.

To me it was interesting.

Being outside Mama's house was always more interesting than being inside.

Action was better than no action.

"You're restless like a little boy," one of Mama's friends told me.

I was already thinking of myself as a boy—so I took it as a compliment.

The girls were inside with their sewing kits and baby dolls.

The boys were outside looking for trouble.

Trouble didn't scare me none. I didn't think twice about it. I figured I could take care of myself.

Rico thought so, too.

Rico was the first dealer who brought me into the game—even though he didn't bring me very far.

Rico was an ultracool cat from New York, half black, half Puerto Rican. Short, handsome, super-smooth.

Loved me some Rico. Rico spotted me right off.

"You just sitting there playing like you don't know what's happening," Rico told me.

I didn't say a word.

"You talk?" he said.

"Sure."

"What do you got to say?"

"Nothing."

A car rolled by with 2 Live Crew screaming from the speakers, "We Want Some Pussy."

"You know what that song's about?" Rico asked.

I nodded.

"I bet you do."

He came closer to me and said, "I got something for you to hold. You cool with that?"

I nodded again.

He handed me a packet. I knew what was inside.

"You put this in your pocket for a minute or two. I'll be back later."

He was testing me.

When he got back in an hour, I was sitting in the same place.

"Got that packet?" he asked.

I handed it to him without saying a word. He handed me three ten-dollar bills.

That was the start.

That was also when the cops wouldn't think that a kid might be holding dope for a dealer. Back then you could get away with it.

Back then, before the New Yorkers like Rico came through, the dope scene was calmer. You'd see people get high, but Rico and his boys raised the stakes: The highs got higher 'cause the dope got stronger. Things got crazier.

The crackheads were really crazy. It was like watching cartoon characters on TV. They had different names—Superman, King Kong, Wacky. If Wacky found a hole—a shop where the

dope was really good—the other fiends would see him trip-
ping and start screaming, "Where the hole at, Wacky?" Wacky
would point to the hole and the crackheads would run over
there to cop. The hole was the spot, the shop where the shit
was sold.

After they got high, they acted all funny, shaking and
dancing and carrying on.

To get the fiends from coke to heroin, which earned
the dealers more money, Rico and his boys would pass out
what they called Ts. Ts were teasers, free samples to get you
started.

"I see you understand the game," Rico said to me.

I didn't even bother to nod. I didn't have to.

The game on the street was so different—more complicated,
more dangerous and deadly—than the games we played in
the schoolyard. The schoolyard games, volleyball and basketball, were great for me because I excelled at them.

I wasn't intimidated by the taller boys who were older
and stronger. I was quicker and more aggressive. I couldn't
be backed down. That attitude earned me a good reputation
in the schoolyard. And my high grades earned me respect in
the classroom. School was cool. School was guarded by security niggas with real guns. School was no joke.

But school was boring. School didn't excite my eyes or
my mind. School was routine. You could predict what would
happen from one day to the next.

On the streets, though, you couldn't predict shit. Might be quiet now, but a minute later, BANG! Something big comes down that changes up the game. The battles over territory, the fight for the best locations to set up shops, the new playas coming in and the old playas going out—the action never stops.

You have to be quick. And smart. If you react wrong, that might be it. If you react right, you can keep playing.

I kept playing.

UNCLE

I was eight years old when I fell in love with Pam Grier.

Mama's grandson was living in the basement where he played the tapes of her movies from the seventies. I was glued to the screen.

Pam Grier was Coffy, a chick with a giant Afro and a body from heaven. She works as a nurse during the day. At night she takes on the bad guys and blows them away, one by one. She's got her own private arsenal and her own style of killing. The poster hanging on the basement walls says, "She's the godmother of them all . . . the baddest one-chick hit squad that ever hit town."

In another movie, Pam is Foxy Brown. This time her hair is curly and her dresses even skimpier. Foxy Brown is so down she don't hesitate cutting off some guy's dick. You don't fuck with Foxy.

But Foxy is make-believe and the streets are real. I can't deal with make-believe for too long. I'm back on streets, just looking around, holding a packet or two, seeing what the day brings.

One day I was sitting on the steps when a man came by. He was in his twenties, good-looking, two golds in his mouth, happy attitude. I knew he was dealing.

"Hey, Snoop," he said, "what you doing?"

"Who's Snoop?" I asked.

"You."

"I ain't Snoop, I'm Fefe."

"No, you Snoop."

"If you say so."

"I say so."

He sat down on the steps next to me.

"You too young to be doing what you doing," he said.

"How you know what I'm doing?" I asked.

"I seen you, Snoop," he said. "I seen you watching this mess out here. You watch like a hawk. You don't miss nothing."

I didn't say nothing.

"You a girl who thinks you're a boy," he said. "But I think you're Snoop."

"Why Snoop?" I asked.

"Snoop out of Charlie Brown. Snoop's that puppy who's always saying cute things. He's sweet but he's sad."

"All right."

"Yeah, you Snoop all right. And I'm telling you you should be in school."

"I am in school. Today's a holiday."

"You do good in school?"

"Real good."

"What subject you like best?"

"Math."

"Figures," he said. "You gotta be good with numbers."

"I am."

"And you're real sure of yourself, ain't you?"

I just shrugged. Where this guy coming from? What did he want? Why was he so interested in me?

His two gold teeth sparkled off the sunshine. He had this big smile across his face. I didn't know what to think.

"What I think," he said, "is that you're smarter than the other kids playing out here. You're one step ahead of them."

I stayed silent.

"Well, in this game it's good to stay one step ahead, but it's even better to stay out completely."

"You out?" I asked him.

"I'm in," he said. "Deep in."

———————

That's the first time I met the man who named me. His name was Arnold Lonly. When I tried calling him Mr. Arnold, like my mama taught me to address my elders, he say, "Just call me Uncle."

And that was that.

Uncle didn't live in the neighborhood but he knew the neighborhood. He worked it. He set up shop and had him a thriving business. From Jump Street, he always had an eye for me. Didn't take long to learn that he really didn't want anything from me. He was just wanted me to stay clear of trouble. He saw something good in me. And I felt his love. He tried to steer me right, but I was gonna do what I was gonna do.

NINE-MILLIMETER

Death lived on our street.

Me and my boy D used to play in front of the Collins Funeral Home, one block down East Oliver, where we'd watch them bring in the bodies. Mr. Collins was a twisted dude.

One day he said he'd pay us to clean out his basement. We backed off, but the promise of money lured us down there. Next thing we knew, old man Collins locked us in.

The room was filled with corpses. One casket was open. A man was in there, and he was still alive. I know because I saw him stretch out his arm and I heard him take his last breath. Frightened to death, we ran up the basement stairs, banging on the door until our hands turned bloody. But old man Collins wouldn't let us out. We finally broke a window and crawled out. I felt like I had escaped death.

Few months later death returned. This time death got all over me.

When it happened, D and I were playing in the alley. By then I was in the sixth grade and running wild—going to every house party I could find and holding packs for the most vicious dealers in the game. Mama and Pop were nice folks, but they couldn't control me. Besides, they had no idea what I was doing.

Me and D weren't doing much that day when two niggas came running down the alley, one chasing the other. The nigga being chased didn't see our bike and tripped over it, falling right in front of us. The nigga chasing him had a gun. Just like that, he pumped four shots into the dude's head.

I watched blood gush out of his skull; I saw his brains splatter out on the concrete.

Never had seen a murder before.

Never had seen anyone shot up right in front of my eyes, inches from where I was standing.

How did I feel?

I can't remember feeling. Just remember looking.

How did I react?

Can't remember reacting. Just remember standing there.

Inside my head I was saying, *Oh, shit, that nigga just got his brains blown out.*

But on the outside I wasn't crying or screaming. I wasn't moving. I was cool as a fuckin' cucumber.

Just stood there.

The killer looked at me, and I looked back at him.

I didn't know what he was going to do, but I wasn't moving.

I wasn't scared 'cause he didn't look like he wanted to shoot me. He already did what he had to do. I think he also saw that, though I was an eyewitness, I was cool. I didn't look like no snitch. I wasn't interested in getting my brains blown out.

So just like that, he tossed the gun at me—a heavy-ass nine-millimeter.

He nodded at me, like it was okay. It was a gift. The gun was mine. I nodded back.

I picked up the joint and put it in the pocket of my baggy jeans.

And that's when everything kicked off.

BOW AND ARROW

In the world of nine-millimeter handguns and semi-automatic weapons, you don't think about bows and arrows murdering someone. Bows and arrows are off some old Robin Hood movie. Who knows anything about bows and arrows?

"Miss M was killed by a bow and arrow," D told me.

"What!" I said. "What you talking about? Miss M is nine months pregnant and about to have her baby."

"Bow and arrow went right through her stomach and into her baby. Killed 'em both."

"That's crazy. Why's anyone shooting an arrow at Miss M?"

"They say it was an accident."

Miss M was the mother of a close friend of mine from school.

I didn't want to believe it. I knew it couldn't have happened. Some fucked-up rumor.

But the rumor wasn't a rumor. The rumor was real.

I went with my friend to the funeral home where her

mother was laid with her little infant. They were both wearing white. They'd taken the child from the womb and placed it next to her mama.

Never seen nothing like that before in my life.

People were screaming with grief, moaning and shouting, "Lord, have mercy!"

I got up and walked by the casket. They were so still.

Mother and child.

Dead.

Silent.

Frozen.

By then I was ten, and I'd seen boys killed. I'd seen men shot down in cold blood. But this here was different. This was a mommy and a baby. This was the saddest sight I'd ever laid eyes on.

My heart was so heavy it was hard to get up when the service was over. I didn't want to leave them alone in that casket. I felt empty. I felt like nothing really mattered if a bow and arrow can go through a mother's tummy and kill both her and the innocent little thing growing inside her.

What kind of world is this?

I didn't have no answers. I didn't want no answers. I didn't want to cry. I could usually keep myself from crying. But not this time. This time I broke down along with everyone else.

This time was the worst.

"YOU BAD"

Boys start humping on girls at a young age. That's just how it is. I started seeing it when I was ten or eleven.

But when they tried humping on me, I fought 'em off. After I beat the shit out of a couple, they left me alone. The boys who understood me became my best friends and running buddies. They looked at me like I was no different than them. In my mind, I wasn't.

Once I had that gun, I was on my way. I hid it under Mama's summer kitchen, a porch in the back of the house where I could crawl under the foundation.

Life went on.

Me and D played basketball with hoops made out of crates. D had game and so did I. He was also tenderhearted, thin-skinned, and hated being teased. When kids at school ganged up on him and started calling him names, he ran to me and said, "Get the joint."

"We don't need to be fooling with no gun," I said.

"I don't wanna shoot 'em, I just wanna whip it out and scare those niggas real bad. Go get it."

I got it. Gave it to D. And the two of us went looking for the boys who'd been ragging on D.

We found them. All ten of them. They saw we were looking for trouble, and they were ready. They had baseball bats and knives, but they weren't ready for a nine-millimeter.

Neither was D. He didn't know how to use it. He didn't distance himself to get good range. He got too far up in their faces. Had no leverage.

"Yo, D," I said, "back up."

But by then he was whipping out the gun. One of the niggas saw what D was doing and knocked the joint out of his hand. Gun fell on the ground. Before anyone could react, I grabbed it. I aimed at the nigga who had plucked it and shot the boy through the leg.

For the first time in my life, I'd fired a gun. The guys backed off. The fight was over before it started. D was all smiles.

"You bad," he said to me. "You ain't scared of nothing."

I got this reputation. And I got this attitude. If anyone questioned what I was doing, I'd say, "What the fuck do you care?"

You feel what I'm saying?

I'm saying that no one cared about me. Mama and Pop were cool, but they were off in their own little cocoon. They couldn't relate to me. They couldn't control me.

I remember looking at Mama while she read her Bible and listened to her gospel music. She'd be smiling and nodding her head to the good grooves. The Word was making her happy. She was a woman who lived the Word. She tried her hardest to put it on me.

"God loves you," she said. "Don't you know that?"

I said I did, but I really didn't. Didn't know who God was.

"God is Jesus," she explains. "He died so you can live."

"I *am* living, Mama."

"He died so you can live forever."

"No one lives forever."

"That where you're wrong, child. Heaven is forever."

"I don't know nothing 'bout no heaven," I said.

Mama smiled and started quoting scripture. The words sounded pretty, but the words didn't mean much to me. I imagined heaven as some make-believe place folks invented to make themselves feel better about living down here in hell.

Pop was the same.

He liked to talk about how Jesus would come down at the end of the world and swoop up all the true believers.

"When is the end coming?" I asked.

"Soon, baby," he said. "Real soon."

"How soon?"

"Could be tomorrow. Could be tonight. That's why we gotta get ready and stay ready."

I loved me some Pop, but I couldn't buy that line. Tonight the sun would set. Tomorrow it would rise. Tuesday would follow Monday and Thursday would follow Wednesday. Same old shit, day in and day out. Far as I could see, no magic Jesus would be dropping out of the sky any time soon.

I couldn't fault Mama and Pop for believing in the magic,

though. The meaning behind the magic was beautiful. But the magic did something to Mama and Pop that removed them from the world—at least the way I looked at the world. They were characters in some goody-goody movie where there's always a happy ending. I liked looking at the movie, but I knew it wasn't for real. I couldn't live in that movie. I was living in another movie—a shoot-'em-up.

Mama and Pop were super-sweet folk, and I know that sweetness must have rubbed off a little on me. But I saw them as two people with their heads in the clouds. They didn't see what was really happening in my world. My world was ruled by street smarts.

If you have them, you survive; if you don't, you die.

That was an exciting idea.

But the idea that Jesus was coming back to get the good guys and punish the bad didn't mean anything. I didn't believe that shit for a minute.

AIN'T NO AVERAGE DAYS

Every day can be a little scary. Or a lot scary.

When I was coming up, fear came early and quick, but I think I musta blocked it or forgotten it.

Some scary shit, though, I ain't ever forgetting.

Ain't ever forgetting the day I was just standing up in the kitchen washing dishes. Mama had just come back from a little vacation. She was upstairs taking a nap. I'd just gotten home from school.

Just your average day.

Until I hear a knock on the door.

"Your cousin home?" asks this nigga standing there. Nigga looks all jittery.

"Who you?" I ask.

"T."

"I'll go see."

I go look for my cousin, who's a man about twenty-one. He's back in the bathroom.

"T is up in here looking for you," I say.

"Tell him I'm in the bathroom."

I tell T.

T says he'll wait.

Meanwhile, I hear my cousin slipping out the back door.

When I look up, T is gone.

I go back to washing a plate.

Then *Pop! Pop! Pop! Pop!*

I drop the plate.

Somone's shooting.

Someone's shot.

Someone's screaming, "Your cousin's down."

Look up the street by Collins Funeral Home. My cousin is laid out on the sidewalk, blood all over him. Homeboys are going through his pockets, stealing his drugs and his money.

Cop sirens are screaming.

Helicopter whirling overhead.

Cousin ain't dead, but he's paralyzed.

It was T who shot him. Later I learned that my cousin had fucked up T the week before, and this was payback.

This was life on East Oliver.

Cousin was running down Oliver to get his piece that he had stashed in another crib. T caught him before he got there.

I think to myself—T could have started shooting back at the house, could have shot me, or Mama, or all of us.

This is how it goes.

Cousin shot. Cousin I loved. Same cousin who always brought me Chinese food. Cousin who liked to get high on weed and laugh with me for hours.

One day Cousin is running around.

Next day Cousin is paralyzed.

Ain't no average days.

"SHE MY DAUGHTER."

When folks asked Mama about me, she'd always say, "She's a good girl. She's a good daughter."

That was Mama. Mama saw the good in everyone.

Truth is, I *was* a good daughter—or least tried to be. Wouldn't ever let anyone say a bad word about Mama or Pop. Anything they asked of me, I did. Willingly.

I worked. Scrubbed floors, washed dishes, did laundry. I liked being Pop's little helper. Liked being Mama's right arm. Liked when Mama told her friends how much energy I had. She was proud of me and I was proud to be called her daughter.

At the same time, you could say I was the daughter of the streets. That was the Snoop Mama and Pop didn't really know. Maybe if they had looked, they would have seen that side of me. But they didn't wanna look. They didn't wanna know. And that was cool with me.

Pops had his cronies who dropped by on some Saturday

nights to drink their beers or sip their whiskey. When I ran through the room where they'd be sitting, Pop would stop me and say, "This here's a fine young girl who's growing up to be a fine young woman."

"Sure-enough," the cronies would say. "You doing a fine job with that child."

All this praise was falling on my head. All this praise was feeling good, except I knew that Mama and Pop had their heads in the clouds.

They missed what was really happening.

For instance . . .

———

One day Mama says we're low on some grocery items. Would I pick them up for her?

"No problem, Mama. I'm on it."

I skip down to the corner store. I got a list and it's taking me a minute or two to tell the man what I need.

Nigga waiting on line behind me says. "Move your li'l ass out the way."

I ignore him, but he leans on me harder.

"Yo bitch, or butch, or boy, or whoever the fuck you are, get moving," he says.

I say, "I'm almost through."

He says, "Butch, you through now."

Then out of nowhere this grown man comes up to the nigga. The man is dark-skinned and tall. He's got on a green leather suit and alligator shoes.

"You best apologize to the young lady," he tells the nigga.

"I ain't apologizing to no fuckin' butch kid," says the nigga.

"I do believe you are," says the man, who pulls out a gun and sticks it in the nigga's ear.

Nigga says, "I do believe I am. I'm apologizing."

"You better show her some respect," says the man. "She my daughter."

That's how I met the man I wound up referring to as Father. He wasn't my real father—I hadn't seen that man since I was three or four—but this nigga was better than my real father. My real father was small-time. My new father was big-time.

Like Uncle, Father was a dealer, but not your average dealer. Father controlled all of East Baltimore. Uncle was in the game. Father *was* the game. Father was King.

Father took a liking to me. I can't tell you why.

Once he gave me fifteen hundred dollars for school supplies.

Another time he took me out to see his mansion that sat way beyond the county line. Looked like something out of *MTV Cribs.* Marble and gold and red silk curtains. Pool tables and Jacuzzis and stained-glass windows.

Father was fast-talking and super-smart. He was nice as he could be to me, and didn't want nothing back. But I heard some niggas say that if you got on the wrong side of Father he'd kill you and your whole family.

Father liked having me around 'cause I stayed quiet and just observed. He knew I was thinking.

"I can hear you thinking," he'd say. "You're thinking one day you'd like having all this shit up in here." He pointed to the circular staircase in the entryway to his house.

I didn't say nothing, but Father was right.

GODMOTHER

"You don't need no gangster godfather," she said. "You need a good godmother. I'm your godmother."

The woman talking was Denise Robbins. She lived right down the street. I was coming out of the sub shop when she was going in. She stopped me to say we needed to talk. I'd known Denise most of my life.

"You know I love my godmother," I told Denise with a smile on my face.

"But you love running these streets more," she snapped back. "Look here, baby, I understand what's happening with you. I see it."

"What do you see?"

"These fools out here, these drug dealers and drug lords, these gangsta godfathers look at you like a mascot. They see you like a pet. To them you're a puppy or a kitten. You think they're protecting you. Ain't that right?"

I just shrug.

"Well, I got news for you, babygirl. Those godfathers only care about one thing—and that's cash money. Maybe they'll reach down and pet their cute lil' puppy from time to time, but they ain't real family. They're hoodlum family. Real family's based on love and caring. Hoodlum family's based on crime and killing. Girl, you better learn the difference before it's too late."

"I know the difference, Denise," I said.

"You say you do, but you sure don't act that way. You're an agitator. You're looking to agitate whenever you can. You thinking agitating is cool. Well, it's not."

"I got people who got my back," I said.

"I know those people," said Denise. "I've known them a helluva lot longer than you. And the gospel truth is that they don't got nothing. They don't have no decency. They don't have no basic respect for human life. They ain't God-fearing and they ain't God-loving. They worship the golden calf. They about money and power. They live by the gun and die by the gun. Is that what you want?"

"I ain't dying any time soon."

"I'm not saying you are, baby. But I am saying that the people you're following will lead you to an early grave. What's the point of that?"

"What's the point of anything?"

"God. God's the point of everything. Comes down to one simple thing—we're here to love each other, not kill each other. In this here neighborhood, you're doing one or the other. I'm saying this not to preach to you, sugar, but just to let you know I love you."

"I love you too, Denise."

"Then I wanna see you change your ways—and change them now. Can I have a promise? Can I have commitment?"

"My sub's getting soggy," I said.

Denise shook her head.

"I want you to think about what I said," she practically begged me. "At least tell me you'll do that."

"I will."

But I didn't.

HE'S THINKING, *SHE TURNED YOU OFF.* I'M THINKING, *SHE TURNED ME OUT.*

Father looked after me from afar.

Uncle looked after me from up close.

Because he was the King, Father was ruling an entire kingdom. Uncle was a Prince with a smaller territory. The King spent a lot of time holed up in his castle, but the Prince was always around.

Uncle had always been convinced I really wasn't gay. He'd been watching me grow up for a few years now and didn't like how I dressed.

"You dress like a boy," he said, "and you act like a boy because the boys are getting all the action. You want some of that action. I understand where you coming from. But if you ever had any real-life sex with a grown woman, you'd get straightened out in a hurry."

I didn't say nothing.

"You don't believe me?" he asked.

I still didn't say nothing.

"All right," Uncle said. "I'll prove it to your stubborn ass. I'll set you up with a horny bitch and see how gay you are after she gets hold of you."

I looked at him, expressionless.

"You think you man enough to handle that?" he asked sarcastically.

I offered up a little smile.

About a week passed.

"I found her," said Uncle when I saw him on the corner.

"Found who?"

"The bitch."

"Oh."

"Here's her address. Go by there tonight."

I went by.

By then I must have been twelve. I'm guessing the woman was nineteen or twenty. She was fine as she could be. I just called her Miss Fine.

"What you know about chopping?" she said to me.

Chopping meant fucking.

"Not too much," I said.

"Ever do it?" she asked.

"Well, not really."

"Maybe you not ready for that. Maybe you ready for this."

For a long while she gave me oral sex. I mean, *a long while*.

Next time I seen Uncle, he was real curious.

He's thinking, *She turned you off.*

I'm thinking, *She turned me out.*

"What did you think of it?" he asked me.

"Well," I said. "It was different."

"I knew you wouldn't like it."

"I didn't say that."

"So what are you saying?"

"I'm saying I think you set me up with a good experiment. And I wouldn't mind experimenting a little more."

Uncle cracked up. "Girl," he said, "you are crazy."

Crazy or not, I went back for more. This time Miss Fine gave me some instructions on the fine art of chopping. She taught me how to strap it on. And it's been on ever since.

Where I grew up, the boys started chopping young. They'd find some wild girls and get them a cheap motel room. The boys would take me along. I was one of them. I was accepted, even in the motel room.

When it was time to chop, I'd strap on but never take off my boxers or undershirt. I didn't have to be butt naked. I didn't want to be butt naked. I could take part and slam as hard as any other boy. And of course I'd last as long as was needed. That was a real advantage.

Another advantage was that Uncle and I never had a falling out, even after he saw that his attempt to change me up sexually wasn't working. He resigned himself to the fact that I was who I was. He never judged me or tried to change me.

I'll always love him for that.

Despite his love and watchful eye, though, there was no slowing me down.

I'm not sure why, but I was hell-bent on working the wild side of the street. The wilder the better.

By the time I hit twelve, I was straight-up out of control.

That's when things went nuts.

DEATH UP CLOSE

I seen death up close when that boy got his brains blown out right in front of me. I seen other niggas get blown away on the streets. When it happens, you stop and look. You stop and think. A life's been snuffed out. That's it. Cat's gone. Ain't never coming back.

Maybe 'cause it happened so much I didn't let myself feel what most people would feel—fear or horror or confusion. I didn't wanna feel too much 'cause if I felt too much I might go crazy living where I lived. So the easiest thing was just to watch in wonder and say to myself, "That's how it go sometime."

I thought I could deal with death. Shit, I *knew* I could deal with death. Death didn't flip me out and death didn't make me scared of the streets. I did all that in spite of the death around me.

But then this one death worked on me a whole different way.

Pop.

One day something needed fixing on the roof and Pop said to me, "Hey, girl, would you mind going up there to fix it."

Didn't mind at all, but Pop always liked going up on the roof. I knew something was wrong.

"You feeling okay?" I asked him.

"A little tired, that's all."

I saw that in his eyes and later asked Mama about it.

"He got a bad report from the doctor" was all she said.

I wanted to ask more about it, but something told me not to.

As weeks went by, he lost weight. Slowed down. Slept during the day. Well, Pop *never* slept during the day. The man was a worker.

Finally Mama said the word.

"Cancer."

Cancer was eating him up, and it was happening fast. So fast that from one day to another you'd see him getting smaller and thinner. Soon he was at the point where he couldn't work at all.

Doctors said he should be in the hospital, but Mama said no. By then she knew he was not getting better. She also knew that he didn't wanna go to no hospital. He wanted to be in his bed at home.

Every night after I came in from running the streets, I'd go in and check on him. He'd be in bed next to Mama. I'd kiss him on his nose. That always made him smile. He'd open his eyes, look at me, and just nod. He was too weak too speak.

Then one of those nights Mama came to wake me up. Had to be around 2:00 or 3:00 A.M.

"Come with me, child," she said.

I followed her into the bedroom. I knew. I felt it. I kissed Pop on the nose, only this time he didn't smile.

His eyes were still open but he wasn't breathing. I took my fingers and gently closed his eyes.

"When the sun comes up," said Mama, "go tell the family. Go tell them in person."

I did like Mama asked me to do. I told everyone that needed telling.

I can't remember crying. Can't remember mourning the man. I knew I loved him and I knew he'd loved me. I was his helper on the roof and in the workshop. He never got mad at me for being a tomboy and never thought I was strange. He took me the way I was.

His being taken away might have gotten me mad. Can't say for sure.

Lots of things got me mad.

Back then, though, I wasn't thinking about how I was feeling.

I was just doing.

"YOU A BOY"

I was doing all I could.

I was running with different crews.

My first crew was all girls. Must have been twenty of them. If I was twelve years old, they were sixteen. All big girls. Big-boned, tall, and strong. I was the shrimp. They let me hang with them 'cause I was nervy. I'd do anything they'd do—and then some.

They weren't lesbians. They had boyfriends. But in most cases they could kick their boyfriend's ass if the nigga got out of line. We called ourselves LMP after three streets in our hood.

We'd go to the movies together and talk to the screen. We tripped on a picture called *Juice* with a rapper who just came out with his first record. He went by 2Pac then and he was something different. He had these eyes and he had this attitude. He had his own flow and burned up the movie screen. Nigga was on fire. *Menace II Society* was another story that spoke our language. Probably the freshest was *New Jack City*. We saw that one until we knew every line. Wesley Snipes chewed that up, Ice T was cold, and Chris Rock had us believing he was a fucked-up crackhead. We were seeing our lives up there.

Day by day, week by week, LMP's little shit got bigger. We got bolder. We started out by mouthing off when other girls came through our territory. Then we got meaner. If a girl we didn't know glanced in our direction, we'd say, "Who you staring at?" Then if she mouthed off, one of my girls would encourage me by saying, "Pop that bitch, Snoop. Pop her hard." I'd smack her in the face or punch her in the jaw. My girls liked to see me fight 'cause I didn't have any quit in me.

What did I have in me?

What the hell was I was so angry about?

I couldn't tell you.

We'd go to a house party and see another girl crew, this one from the west side. They'd get to dancing. LL Cool J had "Mama Said Knock You Out." Dre was rocking *The Chronic*. Or maybe the girls from across town were grinding with our boys to Janet's "That's the Way Loves Goes." Everyone was grinding to that jam. But if the grinding got too sweaty, we'd jump in there and straight-up start throwing the west side bitches out on the street. There were some serious fights, and I don't remember losing any of them.

Because I looked like a little nigga, not a girl, I was a novelty. Sometimes I felt like a mascot. And because I was the youngest and the smallest, I felt privileged to hang with the big girls. But I was always on the outside of the group. My size kept me on the outside, and so did my age, the way I dressed, even the way I walked.

"You a boy," the girls liked to say, "who got born a girl by mistake."

I didn't mind hearing that, but it made me think I really do belong with the boys. So I went back and forth. I ran with both crowds. Both crowds accepted me but both crowds really didn't.

I was in and I was out. I was here and I was there.

Whatever I was, I was hitting the streets hard because nothing was too crazy for me. I could handle it all.

At least I thought I could.

"YOU A GIRL"

Maybe I was always trying to prove what I wasn't—maybe that was it.

Nigga come up to me and say, "You a girl."

I wouldn't say anything back.

He'd shove me real hard.

"You a girl who thinks she's a goddamn boy, ain't you?"

Then he'd shove me harder.

Still don't say nothing.

"If you were really a boy, you wouldn't take this shit off me."

Then he shoved me so hard I nearly went down.

But I didn't. I found my balance and coldcocked the motherfucker.

I heard that question many times—"You think you a boy?"—but never again from him.

Right around then—must have been twelve or thirteen—I got the news from some relative.

"Your mama's dead," she said.

I knew she was talking about my real mother, not the mama who cared for me. I wasn't surprised because I'd seen it coming. Every time my real mother had come by, her eyes were already dead. I could see the life draining out of her. And there wasn't a damn thing anybody could do about it. She was cracked out. It's amazing she lived as long as she did. Finally, her body just couldn't take no more. A kidney disease killed her.

I didn't know how to mourn. Truth be told, I didn't even know how to feel about it. So I didn't feel nothing.

Sure, certain memories of her floated through my mind—the times I met her in the park, the time she locked me in the closet. I thought about her beauty. And how she died the death I'd seen my whole life on the street. Her highs took her to an early grave. I didn't even go to her grave. I don't know where it is.

You'd think her death would have scared me or set me straight. But hell, I wasn't no junkie. I wasn't about to blow coke up my nose and shoot dope in my veins. I wasn't interested in the crack pipe. That shit was for fools.

What interested me was danger.

Going to the edge.

And then over the edge.

I can't tell you why, but at a time when other thirteen-year-olds were buying frilly dresses and training bras, I was buying guns.

I was leaving the LMP crew to hang more and more with the boys.

I was running wild.

Mama saw what was happening. She saw me skipping school for days at a time and coming home late or not at all.

One morning I got home just as Mama was making breakfast. She stopped cooking her oatmeal and gave me a look. Wasn't a hard look and it wasn't a mean look. Mama don't got no mean in her. It was a look that said, *Girl, you breaking my heart.*

"Can we talk, child?" she asked me.

"Sure, Mama."

"You been out there on those streets," she said.

"I'm okay," I assured her. "I know what I'm doing."

"I'm afraid for you, baby."

"Mama," I said, "you don't gotta be afraid."

"I'm afraid I'm losing you."

"That ain't ever gonna happen," I told her.

"I pray for you every night, Felicia. When you ain't home, I pray that angels be watching over you. I pray for your protection, honey."

"I know you do," I said, "and I love you for it."

"I fear those people out there, baby. I fear they turning you the wrong way."

I hated when Mama talked this way 'cause I had no answers. She was right. I *was* being turned the wrong way. I saw it, but I wasn't about to stop it. Something like a fever had come over me. But it wasn't no twenty-four-hour fever. The fever felt permanent. The fever provided chills and thrills. Even when Mama was talking good sense to me, I felt the fever. The fever had more power over me than Mama's warnings.

"When you gonna stop this nonsense, Felicia?" she asked.

"Soon, Mama," I lied. "Real soon."

BONKERS

Mama wasn't the only one who warned me.

Uncle did the same. Fact is, Uncle was always preaching to me.

I remember one afternoon when the streets were slick with rain. We were riding in his Cadillac, going from one of his shops to another. He was making sure his business was straight.

"You gotta get out of this business," he said. "You gotta just think about school."

"I'm thinking about school," I said. "I'm doing good in school."

"You doing good in this business," he said. "See, that's the problem, Snoop. You do good at something you got no business doing."

"Same as you."

"No, ain't the same as me. I'm a man and I know what I'm doing. I got kids. I got money to make. You don't gotta do nothing but study."

"I am studying," I said.

"You ain't studying nothing but these here streets."

He wasn't wrong. And he wasn't convincing. Neither was Father. Fact is, my street shit was getting bigger. I was doing more than just working the corners. I was doing little jobs for operators who needed someone they could count on.

For example, nigga came up to and said, "See that bitch over there, she stole my dope. I want you to beat her ass."

"I ain't killing no one," I said.

"Don't want her killed, Snoop. Just hurt real bad."

"How much?" I asked.

"Fifty now. Fifty when it's done."

I waited a day, followed her down the street, and pulled her in the alley. Pistol-whipped her hard, then beat her with a table leg. Broke her leg and shoulder.

"Satisfied?" I asked the nigga.

He handed me the other fifty, no questions asked.

I was in the back of a stolen car. We pulled up to a gas station. My partner, the driver, started pumping gas. Cops pulled up next to us. The driver got scared and started looking all paranoid. When we saw the cops running our plates, we jumped out of there, tires screeching, cops chasing, chasing us through downtown, chasing us past the fancy houses in Fell's Point, running red lights, jumping curbs, speeding the wrong way down one-way streets, sirens screaming. We dumped the car in a deserted lot and ran like hell. Found an open cellar door, ran down the steps, and kept the rats company for a couple of hours.

Cops never did find us.

Me and my niggas were hired by a dealer to go after some deadbeats. The guys thought they gave us the slip. They went to the mall. They figured with all those shoppers around, the mall had to be safe. They figured wrong.

We followed them past Shoe City. One of them turned and gave us a look that said, "What y'all going to do? Pop us in the mall?"

We popped 'em in the mall.

My little man K did the shooting.

Then there was shooting on the corner of Biddle and Marfat.

I'm walking down the street with my nigga. Just chillin'. Here comes a U-Haul truck. Me and my boy look at each other like this ain't right. The U-Haul truck is going real slow. You don't see slow-moving U-Haul trucks on this street every day. And the driver's looking nervous. I catch his eyes and see something I don't like.

We step back.

U-Haul pulls to the curb.

Back of the truck slowly rolls open.

And suddenly the spraying starts.

Niggas from the west side with nothing better to do than to come east and start spraying.

Fuck those motherfuckers.

Me and my boy duck behind some garbage cans. I pull out my nine-millimeter and blast back. The fools in the U-Haul are sitting targets.

Two of them go down.

They don't touch us.

They run outta there with us still shooting at their asses.

Then there's the graveyard. Seems like we always go to the graveyard. The funeral home and the graveyard.

The graveyard is all foggy this afternoon. It rained in the morning and now a thick fog has moved in. We're there 'cause our friend J was killed by mistake. They killed J thinking he was B. J was a sweetheart. J was our homeboy. B is an asshole. The sweetheart got shot and the asshole is still walking around. B is up there with us telling J good-bye.

We walking toward the grave to bury J when, behind us, we see this guy approaching. We don't know who the fuck he is.

The eyes. The eyes always give it away.

This stranger's eyes are showing nervousness. And before we know it, he starts shooting at B. Shooter was sent to J's funeral to get B, the nigga they wanted dead to begin with.

We say, "Oh, no. Not up in here. You can't disrespect J by turning his funeral into a fuckin' shooting gallery."

My man hits the shooter with a silencer. He goes down slowly, slumped over someone's grave.

We leave him there and go bury J.

A few days later someone catches up with B and shoots him dead.

————————

Wu-Tang Clan is out with "Protect Ya Neck." Later they screaming about "C.R.E.A.M. . . . cash rules everything around me."

Word.

LEAD BAT

Who did I think I was?

Why was I doing what I was doing?

I look back and wonder why.

I look back and ask myself questions that are hard, maybe even impossible, to answer.

But at the time questions weren't part of my life. Questions weren't part of my thinking.

I didn't ask.

I just did.

"What the fuck you doing?" Uncle would ask. "Word out there is that you crazy and getting crazier every day. You got to slow down, Snoop."

"What for?"

"To keep your little ass alive—that's what for."

I knew Uncle loved me. I knew he cared. But Uncle wasn't stopping me.

Neither was Father. I'd see Father roll by in his hundred-thousand-dollar ride. He'd pull over and say, "You staying outta trouble, Snoop?"

"No way," I'd answer honestly.

He'd laugh and lay a hundred on me.

"This is for schoolbooks," he'd say, "and nothing else."

I'd take the money and buy another joint.

Seeing what I saw, being who I was, I knew it was my balls and my nine-millimeters that was keeping me alive.

I wasn't backing down from no one. I wasn't backing down from life.

Life was the streets and the streets didn't scare me none.

———————

Then these dreams. The details were fuzzy but the dreams kept coming back to me. They'd change up, but one thing was always there:

In the dream I'd be driving a car when a lead baseball bat would fly through the window, right at me. I'd wake up in a sweat.

In another dream I'd be walking through downtown Baltimore, kicking it with my niggas, when I'd look up at a lead baseball bat about to crack my head open. I'd wake up drenched in sweat.

There was a dream when I'm in a roller coaster and I look down and see some crazy man beating the controls with a lead baseball bat until the roller coaster starts collapsing and I start plunging to my death. Wake up in more sweat.

I don't understand dreams—then or now. There's nothing you can do about what you dream. But I have to say that in this case those dreams saw something I didn't—until I saw it in the flesh.

This shit was strange.

This was what happened in sure-enough life. This was no dream.

Can't remember the day of the week when it came down. Can't remember the weather. Might have been cloudy. Might have been clear. Don't know what jams were banging back then. Maybe MC Lyte and "Ruffneck." Maybe Da Brat getting "Funkdafied."

I remember that rumors were floating around how Tupac had shot two cops in Atlanta. Tupac might have been on my mind 'cause Pac had just come through our neighborhood.

He knew a lot of the niggas on our block. Couple of weeks before the day that changed my life, I was on the corner when I heard everyone saying, "Pac's around. Pac's down on the Boulevard, Pac's chilling with the niggas." I went down there to see for myself. And there he was.

Beautiful cat. Eyes all bright and lit up with love. Lit up with intelligence. No security either 'cause he knew he was safe with us. We loved Pac. He was short, compact, killer good-looking, and had huge feet. All the big-time dealers came out to see him, protect him, and welcome him.

I got to say, "Whassup, Pac," and see him smile right at me.

His smile was real sincere and his attitude real cool. Seemed like he had time for everyone. I was wishing I could hang with him, but so many people were wanting that same thing. Figured I better leave him alone. Wish him well. Go on my way.

It's something when you see a real star.

On the day when my dream came to life, I wasn't looking for no stars. Wasn't looking for a damn thing. Fact is, I was minding my business, walking my usual walk.

Father once told me, "You don't walk, Snoop. You stalk. You walk like you don't want no one to fuck with you."

"I don't," I said.

So I was stalking through the neighborhood. Forgot where I was going or what I had to do. Doesn't matter 'cause I looked across the street and saw a fight about to come down.

Didn't know the people. Didn't know why they was fighting. Didn't know nothing except fights always drew me. Something about the energy of a fight. The excitement. The danger. I wanted to get close and see what was happening.

So I crossed the street.

I fuckin' crossed the street.

Had I gone straight or turned the corner away from the fight, my whole life would be different.

Funny how so much hinges on five or six little steps.

I took those steps across the street and saw that tempers were boiling over. People calling each other motherfuckers and dirty bitches. Fists were flying.

Then it happened.

The bat.

The lead baseball bat.

A girl looked at me with murder in her eyes. I didn't know her. Never had seen her before. Don't know why she came at me. Made no sense. I wasn't cussing her. I wasn't threatening her. I was just walking by, watching this fighting, when she picked a slugger lead baseball bat—the same bat that had been coming at me in my dreams—and started swinging it at my head. If she caught me, I'd be dead.

I screamed for her to stop, but she wasn't interested in stopping. She wanted to take my head off.

I tried to get away but by then the crowd was too thick. I couldn't move. I was hemmed in by people while this crazy lady was lunging at me with a lead bat.

There was only way to stop her.

I took out my shit. I figured once she saw it, she'd back off. But she wasn't backing off. Even the gun couldn't stop her.

Only one thing could.

Shooting the gun.

Before she got to me, I got to her.

I shot her clean.

My lead stopped her lead.

She fell to the ground.

Dead.

I ran.

MURDER WAS THE CASE

Snoop Dogg said it. Snoop Pearson lived it.

Snoop kept running until she got to one of her niggas' house.

She stayed there for a night. That night she dreamed. Baseball bats were still flying at her head.

In the morning, there was a knock on the door. She peeped through the blinds. Uncle was standing there.

He hugged her. She expected him to cuss her out but he didn't.

"I know what happened," Uncle said. "I done heard all about it."

"The bitch was coming after me with a goddamn bat," Snoop explained. "What was I gonna do?"

"You did what you did," said Uncle. "But now you can't stay here. This neighborhood's too hot."

"Where am I gonna go?" asked Snoop.

"My crib," said Uncle.

Uncle's crib was way 'cross town. Uncle put Snoop in the back room and told her, "You lay low."

Laying low was hard for Snoop. Snoop had to hit the streets. Snoop hated being cooped up anywhere for long.

"If you don't lay low you gonna be cooped up for a lot longer than you can imagine," said Uncle.

"How long I gotta stay here?" asked Snoop.

"Long as I say," Uncle made clear. "Lot of people saw what you did."

"What I did was done in self-defense."

"Whatever you did, the heat's on. Don't move from here."

Snoop had a hard time not moving.

On the television she'd watch *The Cosby Show*. She loved *The Cosby Show*. She pretended like her daddy was a doctor and her mama was a lawyer. Her daddy would say funny things and act the fool, but he'd always be there for her. Her mother was young and beautiful. She'd have all these sisters and brothers, one cleaner than the next. They'd have their little dumb-ass problems like the new dress is too long or the curtains in the bedroom are the wrong color. Snoop would imagine being surrounded by all these people night and day. Nothing could happen to her. Nothing could go wrong.

"Nothing will go wrong long as you keep your ass right where it is," Uncle would tell Snoop soon as he came home from supervising his shops.

"Can't even go out to buy some chips?" Snoop asked.

"We got chips up here in the crib. Stay put."

Staying put meant watching more television.

Reruns of *Mama's Family*. Snoop loved *Mama's Family*. Loved laughing at those crazy white people. Loved how Mama would shoot her mouth off any damn way she pleased.

But how many hours can you watch TV without going nuts?

Snoop would peep out the window. Car rolling by. Snoop Dogg spittin' 'bout "Murder Was the Case That They Gave Me."

Biggie blowing up with "Ready to Die." "Big Poppa" and "Juicy" all over the streets.

The streets were calling.

"Stay inside," Uncle kept saying.

"Just wanna see what's happening," Snoop kept saying.

"I'll tell you what's happening," said Uncle. "They after you."

Snoop stayed in. Four days, five days. Then a whole week. More *Cosby*. More *Mama's Family*.

More dreams.

More nightmares.

Then came the rain, thunder and lightning. Rained like holy hell for days on end.

Cooped inside. Going crazy. Going stir crazy. Rain pounding against the roof. Pounding and pounding and pounding.

Then silence. Sweet silence.

Snoop woke up. It was morning. House was empty. Went to the window. Peeped through the curtains.

Sunshine!

Blue sky!

No clouds! No rain!

Beautiful, beautiful day!

Had to get out.

Just for a minute.

Just for a quick walk to the corner store to buy a little candy bar.

Wouldn't take more than a minute.

———————

Once I was out, I was gone. I was feeling bold. Feeling like they'll never find me. They'll never catch me. I'll duck in this alley. I'll hide behind this van. I'll keep moving so fast, changing up routes and crisscrossing the city, that no one will trace my path.

I had all the moves.

I had all the confidence in the world.

I was so confident, in fact, that I even went back to East Oliver. Stopped by to give Mama a quick kiss. Mama didn't know that I was on the run. She didn't have to know.

"Go by and see your godsister, Monique," said Mama. "She been asking for you."

Monique lived just two doors down on Oliver. I ran by and found her in the kitchen making greens.

She gave me a taste. I love greens.

"Haven't seen you in a while," she said. "Where you been, girl?"

"Here and there," I told her.

I heard the front door open.

"You expecting someone?" I asked.

"Nope."

When I turned, I saw a policeman standing there.

Just like that, I started out the back door. But a policeman was standing there as well.

Nowhere to run, nowhere to hide.

Cop in the kitchen said, "We just wanna question you."

I didn't say nothing.

He approached me with cuffs.

"You gotta cuff me to question me?" I asked.

"'Fraid so," he said.

By then the kitchen was filled with cops. Must have been six of them.

They escorted me out the front door. Now the whole neighborhood was out there. Everyone was looking to see what was happening. There was a whole squadron of police cars.

I could see Mama coming out her front door. She caught a glimpse of me. I saw the hurt in her eyes.

There was nothing I could say, nothing I could do.

MORE THAN
A MINUTE

The Snoop that shot a woman before the woman bashed her head in with a bat, the Snoop that ran and hid, the Snoop that was stupid enough to go out the house, only to be seen and caught—that Snoop was me.

Hard to believe the things I did when I was barely a teenager, but I did them. I watched myself get into this mess, figuring my protectors would get me out.

Mama didn't have no money for lawyers, but Uncle did. Uncle and Father both told me to stay cool, they'd find me the best criminal defense attorney in the city.

I tried to stay cool, but how cool can you stay in the city jail waiting for your case? That shit takes forever.

"How long?" I asked Uncle when he first started explaining about the criminal justice system.

"More than a minute," he said. "There were a bunch of witnesses who saw you shoot."

"Well, I did shoot," I said, "but only to save myself."

"The witnesses might not have seen it that way," Uncle explained. "They might have heard the gunfire and then seen you holding the gun."

"Who knows what the fuck they saw?"

"That's my point, Snoop. I gotta talk to those witnesses."

"How you gonna find them?" I asked.

"I'll find them," said Uncle.

"How long do you think that'll take?"

"I keep telling you, Snoop—more than a minute."

23/1

They had raided Mama's house and taken away pictures of me. They put me on wanted lists and were hunting me down from different directions. I should have known better than to step out like that.

I stepped out and got snagged.

And that was that.

I'd been arrested before, but it was all petty stuff. In and out after an hour or two.

Now my ass was in city jail for God knows how long.

I can't say I was all that scared 'cause most of the niggas in there were boys I knew. Half of them was from around my way. It was like homecoming week.

"Whassup, Snoop," they said. "We glad you gonna kick it with us in here."

I wasn't glad, but I sure as shit wasn't lonely.

Uncle came by. Father too. Both said, "Look here, baby-girl. This here lawyer's coming through to help you. And besides that, we talked to the witnesses and none of them saw you shooting no one. Cops got a weak case."

Whether the case was weak or strong, the case took forever to get going. There were all sorts of delays.

"Delays," said the lawyer, "work in your favor."

Maybe so, but because the judge didn't trust me with no bail, I had to sit in city jail while the wheels of justice turned awfully fuckin' slow.

City jail was boring and bad. Same old damn thing day after day. Go to school in a trailer. Boys on one side, girls on the other. Of course I wanted to sit with the boys, but that was prohibited. The teaching was lame. The teacher was half asleep. The TV at night only got two channels.

I studied my lessons—always did good in school—but that didn't make the boredom go away.

There was no sex, at least none on my part. I didn't know any of the girls well enough to get that close to them. I was getting my survival shit together, and sex was the last thing on my mind.

One thing that was on my mind was escaping. Wasn't my idea, but a girl in my cell called N. Actually, N got the idea from watching *MacGyver*, the TV show about a secret agent.

In one episode, some dude escapes jail through a ceiling. Then he sprinkles pepper behind him so the dogs can't pick up his trail.

"We can do that," said N. "Look up in that ceiling. We

can push back that tile and crawl out to the street, pepper it up and be outta here."

I was skeptical, but what else did I have to do? N convinced me and also convinced S, the other girl in our cell.

N had me to steal some pepper from the kitchen. Then we got us extra blankets and towels we'd use to climb up to the ceiling.

N thought she had her little operation together.

But then S freaked out.

"I ain't doing it!" she screamed. "We'll get caught and get shot."

"Shut the fuck up," I told her.

She wouldn't shut up so I stomped her a few times until she did.

"You don't gotta go with us," I said, "but if you say a word I'll bust you up so bad you won't be able to open your mouth ever again."

I thought that settled that, but I was wrong.

S kept freaking out and a week later wound up telling the CO—the correctional officer—about our escape plan.

CO came by, saw our stash of pepper and stack of blankets and started laughing.

"You fools," she said.

We didn't say nothing.

CO got a stool and pushed back the tile where we'd hope to escape.

"Come on up here," she told me and N. "Look at your escape route."

"I don't need to look," I said. "I know what's up there."

"What?" asked the CO.

"A brick wall thick enough to keep a tank from breaking through," I said.

"If you knew that, why in hell were you looking to climb up there?" she asked.

"I wasn't. We dropped that idea soon as I saw the wall. We innocent."

"Well, you'll have time to think about your innocence when I put you both on administrative lock 23/1," said the CO.

That meant holed up for twenty-three hours with one hour for fresh air.

"But we didn't do shit," I said.

"But you *were* going to do shit," she snapped.

I started to argue, but why?

THE STRIP

I'd never been more than a few miles outside Baltimore. Probably Father's house beyond the county line was the farthest I'd even been.

Never been to L.A. Never seen Hollywood. Other than what I'd seen on TV or in the movies, didn't know nothing about Las Vegas.

So why am I dreaming about that big Strip with all those fancy hotels and their huge neon signs flashing Stardust, Caesar's Palace, the Mirage, and Treasure Island?

Why am I seeing myself in Vegas, shooting craps at the table and playing the roulette wheels?

In this dream, I'm riding around in limos and sipping fancy drinks in the VIP sections of the nightclubs where the rap stars go to chill. I'm sitting in the front row of a heavyweight fight and I'm betting heavy. My man is winning and the crowd is cheering, the money's rolling in, the chips are red and green and yellow and blue, the blue lights of the afterparty are low and I see the faces of all the stars. Mary J. is there.

"That's my wife," I declare. Biggie's there. Faith. Dre. Coolio. Da Brat. Latifah. Nas. Fugees. The party's on and poppin'.

But moving around the room, I feel something's wrong. I don't know what, but my stomach ain't right. My head ain't right. My head is starting to spin. My stomach is starting to ache. I'm feeling sick. Did I eat something rotten or drink some poison?

For all the bad feeling, I keep looking for someone. Don't know who it is, but I gotta find this person because this person is in deep trouble. I leave the party room and run through the casino, run outside on the Strip, run down the Strip, the neon lights racing over my eyes, my eyes searching every which way to find—who?

Everything goes blurry. Everything gets scary. Now there are niggas with knives and guns chasing me and I'm sweating and screaming, "Don't! Don't! Don't!"

"Wake up, girl," says N, who's standing over me.

"Man, this dream freaked me out," I say.

"The way you shaking, looks like a nightmare."

I look at my hands. They are shaking. I don't understand why. A dream has never before made my hands shake.

I try to forget it.

And I do.

———

Can't tell you how much time passed—maybe a few weeks, maybe a few months. But when the news came, I remembered every detail of that crazy dream.

"TUPAC SHAKUR SHOT IN LAS VEGAS."

That's what the news said on September 7, 1996.

For those of us sitting around city jail, it was like the president was shot. Only worse. We couldn't relate to the president. But all of us sure as hell could relate to Pac.

Now I understood my dream. It was so clear. And so god-damn scary.

He was shot in a drive-by and was laid up in some Vegas hospital. Pac was fighting for his life.

The crowd down at city jail wasn't a praying group, but we had us some prayer meetings. We prayed that Pac's life be spared.

We talked about when he was a young kid backup dancer for Digital Underground. We talked about his first record, *2Pacalypse Now,* and his last record, *All Eyez on Me,* and his new joint as Makaveli, *The Don Killuminati: The 7 Day Theory.* We talked about his genius.

We heard his lines in our head: "No matter what you think about, I'm still your child."

"What you feed us as seeds grows and then blows up in your face—that's thug life."

We waited for his change to come. We wanted him to live so bad. We wanted more Pac joints, more Pac movies. We knew he'd blow up to be bigger than anyone in the history of the game.

We wanted him to stay alive.

And then on the sixth day after the shooting, he died. Respiratory failure. Cardiac arrest.

I didn't wanna talk about it. Didn't wanna think about it. Still don't.

———

Uncle came by.

"We gotta talk about your case," he said.

"You were gonna make the case go away," I said. "You said the witnesses didn't really see nothing."

"Well," said Uncle, "almost all of them told us that."

"What you mean, 'almost'?" I asked.

"One witness can't be turned around," he said.

"Man or woman?"

"Woman," said Uncle.

"What's she saying?"

"That she saw you shoot her."

"What does my lawyer say?"

"Your lawyer wants to talk to you."

"Does the lawyer know what he's doing?"

"He's the best. He'll get you the best deal."

THE BEST DEAL

I was up in the gym. I was playing point guard, and I was making all the moves. I'd always been good at hoops, but on this particular afternoon I had a hot hand. Everything was falling.

Game over. I headed back to my cell. Note said my lawyer was there to see me. Cool.

Lawyer was smiling when I came in the room.

"No witnesses will testify against you," he said.

"Word."

"Of course the trial will go on. There's no way we can stop that, but it's pretty clear that their case is weak."

"So you think I'll walk?" I asked.

"I can't guarantee anything," the lawyer said. "But it's looking better than it ever has. Now it all rests on the trial."

I thought about the word "trial."

There's a trial down in the courtroom. Those kinds of trials happen all the time.

Then there's what Mama likes to call the trials and tribulations of life. That kind of trial was already happening with me being locked up in city jail. City jail smelled bad, looked bad, was bad. City jail was a trial of my patience. I saw some niggas lose their cool in city jail and straight-up flip out. They couldn't stop either crying or shaking or screaming shit no one could understand.

City jail was a trial.

———

The trial in the courthouse came up two years after I'd been sitting in city jail. I thought it'd go great.

It didn't.

First day we got there I saw this woman walk in the courtroom with the prosecutors.

"Who's she?" I asked.

"She's the one who said she didn't really see what happened," he said.

"So what's she doing with the prosecutors?"

My lawyer didn't have an answer.

I did.

They'd done flipped her. She was getting ready to testify against me. I could see it in her eyes. I could feel it in her walk. Bitch was ready to do me in.

As the days of pretrial proceedings went by, she walked in the courtroom every day.

I'd seen enough.

"See what kind of deal they'll give me," I told the lawyer.

"You're sure you want to deal?" he asked.

"Sure as shit."

That witness looked clean as a whistle. The jury was going to love her. I didn't stand a chance.

"Cut me a deal," I told my man.

He did.

"This is the best deal they'll give you," he said.

I looked it over and didn't hesitate.

"Take it," I said.

The sentence was reduced down to second-degree murder. They also reduced my jail term down from ten years to eight for the time I'd been sitting in city jail.

Of those eight years, the first five were without parole. That meant that I could be a perfect angel but my ass wasn't going nowhere for five years.

After five there was a possibility of parole.

I was fifteen. Maybe I could get out by the time I was twenty.

Looking at the big picture I felt like I could deal with that.

Five years was a long time, but five years was no lifetime.

I'd adjusted to shit before. I'd adjust to this shit now.

Besides, the move out of city jail was a good thing. I hated that fuckin' place. And from what everyone told me, the joint where I was headed—Maryland Correctional Institution for Women in Jessup—was an upgrade.

They said Jessup was a cleaner, bigger, more modern facility where they tried to actually rehabilitate bitches.

I didn't care about the rehabilitation. I didn't believe in it. I just wanted something better than that stinking sickening city jail.

Jessup was okay with me.

I was eager to get up to the place called the Cut.

A DIFFERENT WORLD

A *Different World* was a spinoff from *The Cosby Show*. Denise Huxtable goes off to college. That's the "different world."

Denise's world was filled with clean-cut college boys and cute little college girls.

I loved the show.

But watching the show from the Cut—which was another world—was a trip.

The inmates had another term for the Cut. They also called it Grandma's House

The Cut sounded hard. And Grandma's House sounded soft.

The Cut was hard.

Like *A Different World*, the Cut had a campus. Only don't look for no wholesome college kids.

Sinbad the comic was in *A Different World*. He was always cracking jokes and making everyone feel okay. We didn't have Sinbad at Grandma's House. We didn't have any happy-go-lucky comics brightening our day with sunshine and laughter. No, sir.

At the same time, the Cut was cool compared to city jail. The Cut had better food—thank you, Jesus—and the Cut had more activities.

Even though I wasn't free, being able to walk from building to building gave me more of a sense of freedom than I felt during those long months I was sitting in city jail.

Also there was a window in my cell. That window was real important. The window overlooked the fields beyond the prison yard and let me watch day turn to night and night turn to day. The window let me study the seasons. It let me see the world, a piece of sky, the foggy mornings, the rain in spring, and the snow in winter. That window opened my eyes to the grass that started growing and the leaves that started falling, the new flowers being born and the old flowers dying, the trees swaying in the storms, the branches broken off by the lightning, the thunder booming in the dead of night with dark clouds racing past the yellow moon.

The window was a beautiful thing.

You might think that sex in a women's prison would be a beautiful thing, too. All those girls cooped up together. They've made movies about that shit. You'd think that me, a sixteen-year-old lesbian, would have the time of my life. Well, you'd be wrong.

In the five years I spent in Grandma's House, I had sex once. Here's why: I value my health. I value my fuckin' survival. The Cut was full of straight-up crazy ladies, fucked-up crackheads, women who had cut off their boyfriends' balls. For real.

I love sex as much as anyone, but I love living more. Early on I saw how romantic relationships in Grandma's House got out of hand. You'd be loving on some woman, then come to learn she belonged to another bitch and wind up with a scissors in your throat. No, thank you.

For romance, I turned to *Guiding Light*. That was my joint, every day at three. I was hooked on that soap and couldn't wait to see what would happen next. It was like *A Different World*. I knew it was fake and had nothing to do with real life. But that only made those shows better. They let you escape from a place where no one was escaping.

I also liked watching Jerry Springer 'cause that motherfucker is crazy. He'll have men on that show who are fucking their mother-in-laws. Then he'll have the daughters breaking chairs over their mothers' heads. All kinds of shit.

So you get in the Cut and you find your place. My place was to fly under the radar. I didn't want to be no star in Grandma's House. I'd rather not be noticed. Why attract attention, especially from the crackheads who were out of their minds and might do anything to you? I stayed to myself.

I played volleyball and was damn good. I overcame the disadvantage of being short by jumping high and spiking hard. We even had a coach from the outside come in and train us. We had big tournaments in the Cut and my team won the trophy.

After I was in there for a month or so, Uncle came to visit.

"You all right?" he asked.

I nodded yes.

"You ain't getting rough with these girls, are you?"

I shook my head no.

"Didn't think so," said Uncle. "You know better than that."

"Sure as hell do."

"What about the schooling in here?" he wanted to know.

"They got a GED program."

"You going for it, Snoop?"

"I think I should," I said.

"I know you should."

He took my hand and patted it.

"Mama been down here to see you?" he asked.

"No, and she's not coming down. I don't want her here. Don't want her to see me in a place like this. It'll break her heart."

"Well, that schooling thing is great," Uncle said. "You'll probably do better in here than you'd do out there. Less distractions."

"Oh, I seen some distractions."

"Well, avoid them," Uncle warned.

"For sure."

For the most part, I did avoid those distractions. Eventually, though, some of those distractions caught up with me.

They had to. No matter how good your intentions, you just can't sit in jail, year after year, and not get your ass in a little trouble. Least I couldn't.

Meanwhile, though, the best entertainment—and the scariest—wasn't the nightmare Freddy Krueger movies they had on VHS. The best entertainment was the stories that women inside the Cut told about themselves. That's some shit I'll never forget.

"I COULDN'T HELP IT. THE MAN JUST HATED KIDS."

You'd hear these stories.

You'd be eating dinner. Or out in the yard. You'd be up in the gym or down in the laundry. The stories you'd hear would burn your ears. You had to listen. You wanted to listen. The stories on TV and the movies were okay. Getting off on *A Different World* or that fool Jerry Springer was one thing; that shit was mildly entertaining. But the real stories told by the real-life women at Grandma's House would blow your goddamn mind.

Of course in jail you had a long time to twist your story any way you wanted. You never knew how true someone else's story might be. But it didn't matter. You sat there and you listened and, after hearing how some lady wound up in the Cut, you just said to yourself, "Lord, have mercy, this bitch is crazy."

No matter how crazy she might be, you sat there and listened. That was the way you passed the time at Grandma's House.

I remember one inmate I'll call L. L was a light-skinned bitch who reminded me of my real mom. She was fine. She had these green eyes that looked like marbles and she had a refined way to talking. When she started into her story, she began telling it like a lady. Like she'd been to college or even law school. She talked like she had no ghetto in her.

"My mother was a schoolteacher," she said. "My grandmother had been a schoolteacher too. My father was a salesman who did very well and I always had lovely clothes. I sang in the choir in the Methodist church and I won all the spelling bees. Even today, I'm a superb speller. My older brother went on to college to become an engineer and I was supposed to go to a fancy college but I began dancing when I was very young. You've probably seen me in the videos. That's how I got out to California—video directors were hiring me. Practically every week I was dancing in a different video. I had an agent, a very important agent, and a famous lawyer who would go over my contracts before I signed anything. I was in demand.

"And I was in love. I don't want to name him, but a famous movie star fell in love with me. He was married at the time, but his wife wasn't interested in lovemaking. She was a social climber and just using him to get to all the parties you read about in the magazines. She didn't love him. I thought I did. I thought he'd build his world around me. That's what he said. That's what the man promised. He took me to Hawaii, to a luxurious resort right there on a private beach. Every day at sunset, the hotel would move the massage tables out by the water and I'd have my massage out there in the open with the breezes from the ocean and that Hawaiian music floating in the air. It was quite something. That's where I learned about skin care products.

"The movie star set me up in business. I was doing extremely well—it was a mail order business—and then I became pregnant. When my first baby came, the movie star left his wife for me. Yes, he did. We moved to a different part of Los Angeles, a very exclusive part, and I became pregnant again. That's when I knew he was cheating on me. But it didn't matter all that much because I'd known for a while that he wasn't the man I'd met in the beginning. He was addicted to gambling, he started getting fat, and his career was going downhill fast. He gave me a settlement for the kids. Big settlement. By then I was fed up with Hollywood. Hollywood is so phony. I wanted to come back to the East Coast where people are more educated and not as crude.

"When I moved back, I had many opportunities to marry. Men have never been a problem for me. There was a banker who wanted to marry me, and there was also a gentleman who owned a chain of fine clothing stores. He bought me a full-length mink coat. I have pictures of me in that coat. I went to New York many times and stayed at the Waldorf, the best hotel in the city, and ate in restaurants that overlooked the river and the bridges. There were very wealthy stockbrokers who wanted to marry me and a man from Egypt who owned factories all over the world. But these men meant nothing to me.

"Then Prince Charming came along. I call him Prince Charming because he was Prince Charming. Tall as a prince. Handsome as a prince. Dark eyes that melted you the minute he looked your way. Big hands and beautiful teeth. Size thirteen shoes. Low, sexy voice like Barry White. He had houses all over the state. A Bentley, a Ferrari, two motorcycles—one white, one black. He had white blood in him, maybe more white than black, because his skin was lighter than mine. He said he had a gold mine in South Africa. He showed me the pictures. He was going to take me there. He said he'd been looking for me his whole life and now that he'd found me, he could never let me go. He was the one.

"We'd talk for hours on end and never got bored. We'd talk all night. We'd love all night. He was one of those men who could control his body. He'd say, 'I'm not coming until you come at least five times.' The lovemaking was like nothing I had ever known. Even now, talking about him gets me wet. He was a man among men.

"He was writing a book about his life and told me, 'Now I have the final chapter. You are the final chapter.' Different businessmen from foreign countries would come to his house for dinner and he'd introduce me as a queen. He gave me a diamond necklace worth eighty thousand dollars. He gave me a gold diamond watch worth fifty thousand dollars. He took me to Florida where a designer custom-made all my outfits and modeled a line after me. The line became famous. The designer wanted to photograph me for his ads, but Prince Charming wouldn't allow it. 'She's mine and mine alone,' he said.

"So my life was perfect. Absolutely perfect. He wanted me to go with him to France for the summer. Of course I loved the idea. But then this one little problem kept coming up: my children. He hated children. He said I couldn't take the children to France. By then, though, Mom had died and all my aunts had moved away.

"'We'll hire a nanny,' I told him.

"'I don't want a nanny,' he said. 'I don't want kids. Kids ruin everything.'

"'I have my kids, though,' I told him.

"'Long as you have your kids, you don't have me,' he said.

"I tried to reason with the man, but he wasn't reasonable that way. He had his attitude. He also had his choice of any woman in the world. I knew that. I saw them coming and going. But I also saw that he was ready to make me his queen. How many women get a chance to be a queen? So I did what I had to do."

L stopped talking. Her green eyes were cold as ice. I didn't want to ask her, but I had to.

"What did you do?" I pried.

"I burned down the house," she said matter-of-factly.

"But it was okay. The children were asleep. It happened so fast they couldn't feel anything."

Wait a second, I was thinking to myself, *this crazy bitch done burned her house with her kids inside? And she's sitting here saying it like it was no worse than overcooking the hamburgers. This is one wack job I'm avoiding for as long as I'm staying at Grandma's House.*

One of the bitches who'd been listening to her along with me couldn't contain herself.

"That's some horrible shit," she said.

"I couldn't help it," said L. "The man just hated kids."

"THAT'S WHY THEY CALL IT GRANDMA'S HOUSE."

I heard a lot of stories about why the Cut started being called Grandma's House. The one that gave me the most chills, though, came down through a woman I'll call Z. I didn't know whether to believe her, but I had a couple of nightmares over her story.

She was in her forties, maybe even older. Had scars all over her face. She'd been cut up and burned something awful. She was ugly to begin with—maybe that's why she was so pissed off at everyone. If you got close to her she'd hiss at you like a cornered cat, so you sure-enough left her alone. No one wanted to fuck with her. There were dozens of rumors about her case but she never talked to anyone. Then she started playing basketball with us. She was over six feet so we put her at center. Even though she was older, she could keep up with the young girls. With the passes I'd feed her, she scored like crazy. That got her to like me.

One day we won a big game because of her inside moves. That put her in a great mood, and she started talking to me. She had a low voice that was scratchy. Even her lips were scarred something awful.

"I know no one likes looking at me," she said, "and I don't give two shits. Fuck 'em."

I didn't say nothing.

"Everyone wants to know what happened to me," she went on. "You wanna know too, don't you?"

Still didn't say nothing.

"Everyone wants to ask me but they too scared. You scared too, ain't you?"

"Hell, yes, I'm scared," I said.

That made her laugh. Made her like me even more.

"Happened when I young. When I was young. My grandma listened to this song that said, 'When I was nothing but a child, all you boys tried to drive me wild.' You ever hear that song?"

"No."

"Old fucked-up blues song. I don't know nothing about those old blues. Grandma would drive me crazy with those old blues. Sounded like shit to me. I don't even like music. Music gives me a fuckin' headache. You like music?"

"I like Pac."

"Oh yeah, Pac. Well, that ain't music. That's poetry, ain't it?"

"Yeah."

"Grandma played her blues music night and day. I hated that shit until I busted up a few of her records. She'd just go out and buy more. She did it to drive me crazy. You know how bitches will drive you crazy."

"Yeah."

"You have a grandmother?"

"Well, I have a foster mother who's like a grandmother," I said. "I call her Mama but she's old enough to be my grandmother."

"You like her?"

"Yeah. She raised me. She didn't have to, but she did."

"My grandmother raised me too," said Z. "My mother up and left after I was born. Just left. How 'bout your mom?"

"Crackhead. She dead."

"Shit," said Z. "That's the stuff that done me in. You ever deal with the pipe?"

"No."

"The pipe is deep. The pipe is so deep until you ain't ever the same again. That's where all these scars come from. You wanna know about the scars?"

"If you feel like talking, I'm listening."

"I'd pick me the meanest motherfuckers to get high with. Don't know why. But every last one would be lowdown and nasty. When we run out of shit, they'd make me chase after more. I'm the kind of bitch who'd say, 'Fuck you. *You* chase after the shit.' They'd cut me. I'd cut 'em back. They'd cut me again. And that's how it go. Went that way for years. But the thing about the pipe is that the pipe takes you all the way down to places you didn't know were there. You been to the crack house?"

"I've been by to take a look."

"So you know what's happening in there."

"I have some idea," I said.

"Well, if you hanging in the crack house, you okay. That's the nice part of it. That means you getting loaded and you cool. It's when you don't even have enough money to buy nothing in the crack house—that's when you fucked up. That's when you out on the street doing stick-ups and shit. Doing anything to get you some money to buy some crack. You feel me?"

"Oh yeah," I said. "I seen that my whole life."

"Well, you ain't seen nothing like what happened to me. I done so many stick-ups in my neighborhood there was no one left to stick up. So I started robbing my grandmother. Ain't that something?"

"You ain't the only one," I said.

"But I'm the only one who took it as far I took it."

For a couple of seconds, Z fell silent.

"How far is that?" I asked her.

Z took a deep breath and went on. "She and her three friends play poker every Friday. Penny poker. Her three friends, they grandmas too. Old bitches. They be sitting in there listening to those blues records and playing their little card game. One of those Fridays I came into the house looking for Grandma's purse. I find it in the bedroom and start snatching out her money. One of the old bitches sees me and starts yelling. Grandma gets up and tries to stop me. I ain't in my right mind. I'm in my crack mind. Grandma starts smacking at me. I smack her down. Knock her down. The other bitches start screaming."

Z stopped again. Her eyes got funny. She took all these deep breaths.

I didn't say a word. Nothing I could say.

"I cut her throat," she finally said.

I just nodded.

"Killed my own fuckin' grandma."

"That's really something."

"That's why they named this here joint after me. That's why they call it Grandma's House."

GG

Called her GG because she wore everything Gucci. Gucci belt, Gucci shoes, Gucci sunglasses. For all we knew, she wiped her ass with Gucci toilet paper.

In real life GG had been a Gucci whore pimped by a cat she called Valentino. Valentino was notorious for training his girls to rob their johns. This here was the story GG told me:

"Valentino was known as the man who couldn't come. That's why he was so beloved by his women. They'd be popping off like firecrackers and Valentino, well, he'd be as fresh as when he started. A half hour, an hour, I've seen him go ninety minutes on three different bitches. Didn't make no difference to Valentino. The porn people were all after him, but he said, 'Fuck y'all. Y'all can't match the money I'm making out here running my girls.'

"See, to be a Valentino girl was a way to get famous. He didn't choose just anyone. You had to have class to start with. The right look, right goods, right everything. Once you got the nod, though, that was just the beginning. Then my boy would school you. School you hard but school you right. He'd tell you about johns. When they bumpin' you, some of 'em wanna last. Some of 'em don't. Here's how to make 'em last. Here's how to pop 'em right quick. Valentino would school you on psychology. The man's a genius. See, psychology is what it's all about. Getting inside a motherfucker's head. If the john want Mama, give him Mama. He want a schoolgirl, you be a schoolgirl. He dreaming of Halle, start purring like Halle. Valentino had this saying, 'Know your john, double your earnings.' Valentino was right.

"Problem was, Valentino had him some expensive taste. Loved the big cars and the big cribs and even got him a big boat somewhere out there on the bay. The boat had a captain and a cook. I know 'cause I was about the only working bitch who done seen that boat. Boat was seriously tricked out. Looked like a church with all the marble and gold on the walls. But paying for that marble and gold became a problem for Valentino. He got himself squeezed between two hard-nosed money men. He needed serious cash.

"That's when Valentino changed up his game. Game used to be, 'Some guy fucks you and you get paid.' Now the game was, 'Some guy fucks you, and while he's fucking you, Valentino has a dude sneak in the room to take his money.' So my job is to scream so loud during the fucking until the john can hear nothing but my fuckin' screaming. That's kinda fun. But when the john sees what's happening in the middle of the fuck and jumps off me, I'm supposed to knock him over the head with a chair. I'm no good at that. I don't like it. 'Tough shit,' Valentino says, 'You'll do it.' Did it for a while. More I did it, though, more I hated it. Some guy wanna fuck me, cool. But I don't wanna fuck him up. See, I'm one of those nonviolent people like Dr. King was talking about. I'm tired of smacking motherfuckers upside the head. I refuse. 'Fine, bitch, then I'll smack *you* upside *your* head. How you like that?' I don't like it. Don't like it one bit, but Valentino's getting rougher and I'm getting sorer and the shit's getting crazier until one night I got a rich john up in there and I ain't screaming loud enough to drown out the noise of the man robbing the john. The john sees what's happening and jumps off me right quick. That's when I'm supposed to crack him over the head, but I ain't playing. He and Valentino's man get into it. Valentino's man ain't fucking around. He up and shoots the john through the heart. Just like that, we got us a dead body on our hands.

"Valentino's all pissed. Makes me help bury the john out in the country somewhere. That gets me pissed. Cops come round looking for the dead guy. They start pointing at me. But I ain't pointing at no one. I ain't saying nothing. But then they start getting serious with first-degree murder charges and I start pointing to the place where we buried the man. I get accessory to murder. That's a helluva lot better than first degree. I get to come to Grandma's House and chill for a minute."

"How 'bout Valentino?" I want to know.

"Money men who was squeezing him dealt with him."

"And did what?"

"What do you think? Squeezed the fuckin' life out of him."

DILDOS FOR SALE

Doing business at Grandma's House is a different deal. It ain't like setting up a Starbucks in the mall.

The girls have different needs and, if you're interested in making cash, you will find a way to supply those needs.

What does everybody need at Grandma's House? What does everyone want?

Sex.

So I started thinking about sex—not for myself, but for my business. I was still too cautious to get crazy with sex in the Cut. But sex was happening all around me and, as someone used to hustling one kind of merchandise or another, I was trying to figure out how to combine commerce and sex.

What kind of merchandise did the girls need most?

Dildos.

Whether bi, straight, or straight-up gay, women want it; or they want to give it. Anyway you look at it, they need it.

And since the Cut didn't exactly have a gift shop that sold

sex toys, I figured I'd set up my own. I also figured that I'd keep it simple. One product and one product only. The essential product. The ever-popular dildo, the product that never goes out of style and is always in demand.

Problem is, where do you get them? Who do you order them from? Who's your supplier?

I saw that I had to be my own supplier. And with that in mind, I'd find my way into the medical supply room to get some Ace bandages. Ace bandages are the building blocks to a good sturdy dildo. If the supply room was closed off, I'd fake an ankle injury and get me some bandages through the nurses.

I took orders.

I crafted them in four sizes—small, medium, large, and extra large. Made them as real-life as possible. Took me a few hours to make a real good one. I knew my workmanship had to be solid or I'd get complaints. Not to brag, but all the time I was in business, never had one complaint. Word went out— "If you need a do-right dildo, see Snoop."

Payment would come in different forms. Sometimes cans of soup. Sometimes packs of cookies. Sometimes candy. You couldn't get rich in the Cut, but you could keep yourself busy.

My dildo business was a good thing.

One girl loved her fake dick so much she gave me a gift. A fat joint. I'm no pothead, but it's easy to get bored at Grandma's House. I looked at the joint and said, "Hell, why not?"

THE TRIP

Just one joint—one little innocent joint. A simple commonplace cigarette stuffed with commonplace marijuana.

Or so I thought.

I didn't have a lab to analyze the shit. Maybe it was something more than pot. Or maybe a strain of pot grown to fuck you up for good. Who knows.

But there I was, sitting out in the yard after having done my clean-up duty early. I had about a half hour to kill. The afternoon was windy. Some of the girls were playing basketball, but I was feeling tired. And the joint this bitch had slipped me was looking pretty good.

Why not?

Off in the corner of the yard, no one was looking my way. Besides, I wasn't known as a troublemaker. None of the guards gave me attitude.

Lit it.

Sucked up the smoke.

Kicked back and watched the clouds roll by.

Cool.

Clouds are cool.

Weird, but one of those clouds looked like an angry old man. I could see his eyes and his mouth. His motherfuckin' mouth was moving. I seen it moving. There was some thunder, but, wait—wasn't thunder. He was talking. Saying something. But what? Holy shit, I could make out his words. His words were, "Snoop, you getting high. Snoop getting fucked up." The thunder was talking. Thunder can't talk, but I'd be goddamned if I didn't hear it again.

Then I seen the girls playing basketball look at me. They heard the thunder. They knew I was high.

Better take another hit.

Took another hit.

Deeper hit.

Kept that shit inside. Held it. Let it swim up through my brain so it could straighten out my thoughts. But my thoughts were getting more crooked with every puff. My thoughts were saying, "The sky is screaming your name. Get your ass inside."

So I finished off the joint and went inside. Went to my cell and sat there, eyes closed, trying to see pretty pictures and hear pretty music. Instead I heard this chanting. Sounded like all the bitches in the Cut were chanting my name, saying, "Snoop's high. Snoop's high. Snoop's high." When the guarded passed by my cell, she looked at me like she knew.

Everyone knew.

I'd been high before, so I realized paranoia is part of being high. But for some reason I couldn't call this paranoia. I had to call it the truth. This was real. The chanting was real. I heard it distinctly. Came right at me.

I put my hands to my ears but the chanting got louder. When I tried to lie down on my bunk, my skin felt all bumpy. I was getting bumps. I'd study one bump and it looked like it was getting bigger. Bumps all over me. Bumps and that fuckin' chanting. I started itching. Started scratching. Bumps started blowing up. Looked in a mirror and saw my eyes bulging out. Felt like my goddamn eyes were about to pop out of my face.

Now I was getting scared.

Now I wanted the high to stop.

But I was still going up, not down, and the chant had turned into screams—bitches screaming my name—and the screaming wouldn't stop and I went to the bunk and curled myself up like a baby and started crying to myself, crying 'cause I was scared I wouldn't come down from this fucked-up high, crying to myself 'cause I was scared to cry out loud 'cause I was ashamed of crying and ashamed that a lousy joint had wacked me out.

I was crying when a CO came in the cell and saw me there.

"You okay, baby?"

I looked up at her. She was pretty. Her eyes were soft.

I sucked in my breath and tried to act strong, but she saw me falling apart. She put her hand on my forehead.

"You gonna be all right," she said. "Sometimes it just gets that way in here. But it'll pass, sugar. You'll be fine."

I let her touch me. I liked her touching me. I liked when she held my hand. Didn't want to tell her that I was high on some crazy weed, but I figured she already guessed that. She didn't care. But she did care about me. She sat with me for a long spell. When I started shaking, she held me.

"I'd take you to the clinic," she said, "but you're better off here. They'll give you blood tests in the clinic. You don't want no blood tests."

The CO was a sweetheart.

That night she became my sweetheart.

That night she got me through the worst trip of my life.

CO became my first and only love in the Cut.

CO

Falling in love in Grandma's House is a different kind of falling in love. You're not in the world. You're in jail.

You ain't going to the movies and ice-skating or taking a walk in the park. You'd like to snuggle by the fireplace or book a room at the Hotsheet Hotel. But there's no fireplace and not much time to snuggle. You got to sneak, and sneaking ain't easy in the Cut.

Truth is, me and CO never did make love. We made out. We kissed in the dark corners and found some time for hugging, but straight-up screwing never happened. Neither of us wanted her to get fired. That would be the end of our relationship and the end of the only romance I was having.

CO did me favors. One big favor was getting me a bunch of colognes and perfumes from the outside so I could sell 'em on the inside. Had me a good little business going.

Bitches all over Grandma's House came to know me as the perfume lady. Had me a bunch of different brands—one for every taste.

CO was a lady. Naturally I was the man in the relationship. I would have loved to have been fucking CO, but just the idea that another woman was caring about me and loving on me made a difference. She'd slip me little notes that told me to meet her here or meet her there. Then she started writing letters about her life on the outside. How she was lonely. How she'd never met anyone like me. How, once I got out, she could see us hooking up forever.

"You mean it?" I said.

"With all my heart."

But hearts are changed by the Cut. Once inside, you don't have the same heart you had on the outside. Least I didn't.

At age eighteen, my heart had hardened.

It was hard to begin with, but seeing what I saw and hearing what I heard, my outlook on life got even more basic: Life was shit. So fuck it. Get what you can.

I know that folk talk about rehabilitation in jail, and for a while I thought maybe I'd become a different person. But forget about it.

Maybe if I had had a good teacher to inspire me—maybe that would have made a difference. But the truth is that I had this one teacher who made my life miserable. She had the opposite temperament of CO.

She had it out for me. She called me all kinds of things.

But I had only word for her . . .

BITCH

Bitch look at me and say, "You got your homework?"

"Yeah, I got my homework."

"Read it."

I read a little essay I wrote about basketball players.

Bitch say, "I didn't tell you to write about basketball."

"You said to write about what I like on television."

"Television *shows*," Bitch says, "not television sports."

"Well, a game is a show."

"Tear up your essay."

"What!"

"You heard me—tear it up."

"But I wrote it real carefully."

"You wrote it real sloppy."

"How you know that?"

Bitch say, "'Cause everything you do is sloppy. Now write a new essay and present it in class tomorrow."

I look at the bitch like she's crazy.

Problem is, I believe she's crazy in love with me. I truly believe she likes girls, and she has the hots for me in particular. But because she don't like liking what she likes, she takes it out on me. She knows I ain't ashamed of being gay. I like it. I'm proud of who I am. Meanwhile, this bitch is scared of who she is. So she makes life in Grandma's House miserable for as many girls as she can.

Next day I come into class with something I wrote about *The Fresh Prince of Bel-Air.*

I say something about how Will Smith has a funny point of view that makes everyone laugh, regardless of whether they're rich or poor. He's a homeboy that everyone loves.

Bitch says, "You missed the point."

"So what *is* the point?" I ask.

"The point is the contrast between life in the affluent suburbs of Los Angeles and the ghetto attitude of a boy from Philadelphia."

"Isn't the point that Will's funny as hell?" I ask.

"But what's underneath the humor?" Bitch asks.

"What's underneath your piss-ass mood?" I ask.

"I'm going to have to cite your negative behavior," she says.

I say, "I'm going to have to cite your lousy sense of humor."

"You're making it worse for yourself."

"You ain't helping none, bitch."

Bitch say, "That does it."

I say, "I hope so. You kicking me out of here?"

Bitch say, "No, you're not getting out of the final exam."

I took her fuckin' final exam and got all the answers right. Except she changed my answers around and failed me. She rigged it to make it look like I didn't know anything.

On top of that, she reports me to the supervising administrator.

"Your teacher feels that you're uncooperative and disruptive," says the supervisor. "Plus, you failed the exam."

I say, "Fuck that bitch. She switched my answers to *make* me fail. She's a dyke who don't know it. That ain't my fault."

Supervisor tells me I have to change my attitude or I'll never get my GED.

"Fuck that too," I say.

And with that, I go back to my cell.

That damn teacher sets off a bad period for me. For weeks afterward, I skip my classes. That teacher turns me against book-learning.

I go through this heavy-duty anger period.

I see anger all around me.

Old woman inmate who been living in the Cut for years gets angry at her cellmate. Cellmate won't stop talking shit. Cellmate badmouths this old woman night and day.

Then one day in the rec room, the old woman throws a pot of boiling water at her cellmate and disfigures her face for life. That stops the bitch from talking shit.

I get angry at my own cellmates.

One of my cellmates says I gotta cut her hair. I don't wanna bother with her hair.

"You got to," she keeps saying. "I seen how you cut that other bitch's hair and I liked how it looked. Now cut mine."

I can't get her to shut up, so I figure it's easier cut her god-damn hair than listen to her yap.

I do it. I design a little style for her.

But she hates it.

"You got me looking like Mr. T," she says.

"I like the way it looks," I tell her.

"You did it to spite me," she says.

"Fuck you. You were the one who kept after me till I did it. Well, I've done it. This ain't no beauty salon up in here."

"Fix it!" she starts screaming. "You gotta fix it!"

"I don't gotta fix shit."

"I ain't going out there looking like Mr. T."

"Exactly where you going?" I ask. "You in prison, bitch. Ain't nowhere *to* go."

"I'm telling you to give me a different cut," she keeps saying.

I'm through arguing. I start walking away. She grabs my arm.

"Let go," I say.

She won't let go. I pull away.

Then she makes a mistake. Big mistake.

She slaps me.

I see red. I go off. I take the clippers and go across her face. She starts shrieking. Blood everywhere.

She never asks me to cut her hair again.

Supervisor calls me in again.

"You're going to have to do something about your behavior."

"What?" I ask.

"You tell me."

"I don't know," I say.

"You mess up in school. You cutting up your cellmates."

"That one cellmate was fucking with me. That's the only reason I cut her."

"You're headed for more time not less. Is that what you want?"

"I just wanna be left alone," I say.

"And I want you to correct your conduct."

I roll my eyes up and study the ceiling.

"Look," says the supervisor, "is there someone from the outside you'd listen to? Your mother, for example."

"She dead."'

"Your stepmother."

"I don't want her here. I don't want her to see me in this mess."

"Anyone else?" she asks.

I think for a while.

"Call Uncle. He can talk to me. Uncle can talk to me any time he wants to."

BRAIN DEAD

Sitting there across the table from me, he looked beautiful. He put a smile on my face.

"Girl," he said, "looks like you haven't smiled in a while. Looks like they done turned you mean in here."

"Why you say that?" I asked.

"That's what they told me."

"Who told you what?" I wanted to know.

"The supervisor said you turned against your classes and turned against your teachers."

"One teacher," I said. "One bitch that has it in for me."

"Why's that?" Uncle asked.

"Closet case. She hates that I'm out and she's in."

"Sounds like you've been taking psychology classes," Uncle said.

"I don't need no psychology to see what she's about."

"Whatever she's about has nothing to do with what you're about."

"That's what I'm saying," I said.

"That's what you're saying but it ain't what you're doing," Uncle explained. "What you're doing is fucking up your education over one teacher. That don't make good sense, does it?"

"I don't need to kiss anyone's ass."

"I ain't telling you to kiss ass, Snoop. I'm telling you that you've been in this place two, three years already. You're eighteen years old. You'll walk out of here in another couple years. You'll walk out educated or you'll walk out brain dead. That's what it comes down to."

"The Cut will kill off your brain cells no matter what."

"Not if you change your attitude it won't," said Uncle. "Right now you're all negative up in here. You done made that choice. No one made it for you."

"Except the bitch," I said.

"The bitch is a bitch. That ain't gonna change. But how you react to the bitch is up to you. You can let her throw you off or you can go your own way."

"What way is that?" I asked.

"Well," said Uncle, looking at me square in the eyes, "there's only two ways. Up or down."

"And you saying I'm going down?" I ask.

"I know it. I see it. You got to check yourself, girl, or you don't got a prayer. You'll get more bitter by the day, and by the time you look around you'll be nothing but a crazy angry bitch yourself."

I started to answer back, but Uncle stopped me. He said, "Just think about what I'm saying."

I thought about that expression "brain dead."

Who the fuck wants to be brain dead?

"You serious about this brain dead shit, ain't you?" I said to Uncle.

"Serious as a heart attack, baby. You got to take advantage of what this place got to offer. If you can get your GED inside here, grab it. You'd be a fool not to."

We spent another half hour or so talking 'bout what was happening back on the block.

"You all right?" I asked uncle. "The shops in good shape?"

"The shit is always crazy," he said, "but you don't gotta worry about that. You just gotta worry about keeping yourself in good shape. You a jewel, Snoop. You a valuable jewel. When you get outta this joint, you gonna shine."

I had to hug the man for saying that.

I had to hug the man for coming down to the Cut to set me straight.

No one else could do that except Uncle.

LOOKING UP

Uncle was right.

Up's better than down.

Looking down you see nothing but concrete.

Looking up I see that window.

I look out that window.

Little buds are popping out all over the branches of the trees.

Soon the buds will burst open into leaves.

Soon spring will be warming us up.

Flowers will start blooming and things will smell sweeter.

Longer days, brighter light, more time to play in the yard.

In the Cut, winter's a motherfucker. Spring's a breath of fresh air.

Winter can make you crazy. Spring can make you hopeful.

After Uncle's visit, I was ready to get hopeful.

I needed that turnaround. I needed to put myself on a

sensible course of learning something besides making dildos in three different sizes.

I needed Uncle's energy and the knowledge that he really cared for me, no matter what kind of mess I got myself into.

I needed all the help I could get. Some of that help came from another piece of good news. This one was a surprise. I learned that my godmother, Denise Robbins, another big supporter of mine, had trained to be a correctional officer and was coming to work at the Cut. Denise was family and having family inside Grandma's House couldn't help but keep my spirits high.

She couldn't do me any special favors, but just seeing her from time to time did me a world of good.

Denise was another reason I started to turn the corner from negative to positive.

Around this time, a negative came up.

Word came down that the mother of the girl who had gone after me with a bat—the girl I killed—was being sent down to the Cut. Word came down that the woman would be looking for me.

I wasn't worried. I knew at Grandma's House they put people like that in protective custody—and that's just what they did with her. The woman had a lot of emotional problems. From time to time, I'd see her pass by, but she was always with an officer. She never said shit to me, and I never said shit to her.

Did I feel bad about what I'd done to her daughter?

Of course I did. I felt horrible about it. I felt deeply remorseful. If there had been some way to undo it, I would have. But in my heart I knew that what I'd done was done out of self-preservation. It was kill or be killed. There was only way to save myself—and that's what I did.

The women in the Cut knew what was happening. They kept the girl's mother away from me and, for the most part, out of my sight.

So I went my way without fear.

I kept my head up, my eyes open.

I went back into the classroom, where the teacher no longer bothered me. She tried her best—she was still a bitch—but, after Uncle's visit, I was a different person. I wasn't taking none of the bitch's attitude personally. She could dog me all she wanted. I didn't care. I was reading deep into the books. I was learning my lessons. I had the answers before anyone else. History class. English class. Math. You name it. Snoop was on the case.

When I met CO in a secret alleyway where no one could find us, when I held her in my arms and gave her a kiss, when she told me that she loved me and was proud of the progress I was making, I said, "Baby, everything's changing now. Everything's changing for the better. This here is the best day of my life."

THE WORST DAY OF MY LIFE

When my dreams start getting crazy, I start to worry.

I'm not saying I can see the future. I can't. But I pick up vibes and those vibes creep into my sleep.

For weeks my sleep was disturbed. I was dreaming of bad shit. Can't remember it all, but it had something to do with knifings and shootings. Crews were being ambushed and sprayed. Then there were storms, hurricanes, tidal waves, and tornadoes blowing through the neighborhood and wiping out everything in their path.

I'd wake up sweating. Wake up wondering. Wake up with this bad feeling in the pit of my stomach.

Oh, well. There was work to do. I was on the cleanup patrol in the yard. I had my books to read and my lessons to learn. I had to keep my nose clean and stay outta trouble. I couldn't think of the other twenty or twenty-four months

I had to go, just sitting in Grandma's House. I had to get up and do things to make the time pass. I had to live the life of the Cut.

And I did.

I'd see bitches about to get in a fight, and I'd avoid them.

Bitches might threaten me. I'd ignore them too. I couldn't be provoked into a fight. Had no reason to fight. Had every reason to keep moving up.

So where were these dreams coming from?

In one, I'm walking through an open field and bombs are dropping on my head.

In another, a pack of wolves are chasing me down.

I'm drowning in the ocean and I'm being pushed out of a skyscraper.

I wake up with a headache, every single day.

The headaches get worse. Aspirin don't help. Advil don't help. The Cut has a pretty good doctor, but she says there ain't nothing wrong with me. She says everyone in jail gets headaches.

Then one day I'm looking out that little window in my cell and see dark clouds coming over the horizon. They coming fast. It's a storm from hell. Before I know it, day's turned to night, pitch-black night, and the thunder's booming and the lightning crackling and it sounds like God is dumping his anger down on Grandma's House. Feels like the ceiling's about to collapse and the walls above to cave in.

I'm walking down the hallways, on my way to the rec room, with the shit just getting louder and louder, when I see a girl on the phone. I know her from the neighborhood.

She puts down the phone and says to me, "Snoop, I just heard about Uncle. I suppose you know already."

"Know what?"

"He dead."

"What you mean dead?"

"What part of 'dead' don't you understand? The mother-fucker ain't breathing no more."

"He ain't dead," I say. "He was just here visiting me."

"He dead all right. Drug deal went bad. The word is that he went to drop off two bricks and some nigga turned on him. Shot him up real bad."

I look this bitch in her eyes. I see she ain't lying. But I also know that I can't deal with the truth.

I go through something strange.

I tell myself this ain't happening.

I haven't walked down the hallway.

I haven't seen homegirl talking on the phone.

She didn't look at me.

I didn't look at her.

She didn't open her mouth.

She didn't tell me nothing.

She didn't say Uncle's dead.

Uncle's not dead.

Uncle's alive.

None of this happening.

Uncle was just here visiting me. Uncle gave me good encouragement. Uncle gave me the word I needed.

He'll be back to visit. Maybe next week. Maybe the week after.

Everything's cool.

When I get out of here, first thing I'll do is run over to Uncle's crib. He'll be there with his wife and kids. He'll greet me with that big smile of his. We'll hug. We'll sit down to lunch and he'll tell me how proud he is of me.

It'll be beautiful.

Uncle's beautiful.

Uncle's not dead.

He can't be.

It didn't happen.

LOSING IT

It did happen.

It took me a few minutes, and I was back to reality. Homegirl had told me that Uncle was dead. Her words were true, and just like that, I snapped.

I ripped the pay phone from the wall and threw it on the cement floor. Then I threw myself on the floor and started screaming.

Never in my life had I ever gone into this kind of rage: hitting my head on the floor, hitting again and again until I passed out.

Later they told me that the Turtles—the armed guards who worked at Grandma's House—had to haul me off. It took four of them to contain me. When I woke up, I was in the mental ward. The way I was acting, they were scared I'd kill myself. And they weren't wrong to be scared.

If it weren't for the good-hearted guards that stayed by my side and saw me through, I might have done just that.

But those guards were like the doctors who saved me when I was a cross-eyed crack baby. They got me through some of the worst days and nights of my life.

I can't remember everything that was going through my mind during those long hours. I know it was despair, and depression, and anger, and confusion, and heartbreak, and fear. I was afraid that I couldn't make it without Uncle. Uncle had been the rock. Uncle had been my biggest believer.

Despair said that nothing was right in this world. Depression said that nothing would ever get better. Anger said that the world was fucked. Anger cursed a world that would kill Uncle in cold blood. Confusion said nothing made sense. Heartbreak said something sweet and good was gone and would never be back. Fear said that what happened to Uncle could happen to me. *Would* happen to me.

CO tried to comfort me. She came to the mental ward and, when no one was looking, she held me. CO told me I'd get through it. CO was cool.

I was anything *but* cool. I was sweating at night and freezing in the morning. I had the chills. The killer headaches came back. The nightmares got worse. I kept thinking—*If Uncle's dead, why should I be alive?*

You can only stay in the mental ward so long. You can only take sleeping pills and tranquilizers for so long. After a while, the pills turn on you and the tranquilizers get you crazier than you were before. So you have to make up your mind. As Uncle put it, ain't but two ways—up and down.

I was going down.

When I got out of the mental ward, I felt myself going down. In my cell, I looked out the window. When the sun was shining I hated the sun because it made things look good when things were bad. When the sun went away it reminded me that there was no sunshine in my heart. When I looked out the window at night I couldn't see stars, only darkness.

I went about doing what I had to do, lining up, mopping up, eating a little bit of this and a little bit of that. I lost weight. Refused to play basketball. Barely knew where I was or what I was doing.

Went through the paces.

Didn't see no light, no hope, no nothing.

DOUBLE WHAMMY

Couldn't do the usual things that got me going.

Couldn't watch TV.

Couldn't read a book. Or a magazine. Or even the sports page in the newspaper.

Couldn't talk to anyone.

Couldn't listen to anyone.

Could hardly look at anyone.

Kept my eyes glued to the floor.

Kept my mind glued to Uncle.

Him getting shot. Him being dead. Him never coming back.

My mind was fucking me, getting me to remember the good times when Uncle first became my friend. When he'd give me all that good advice. When he'd stop by the corner to make sure his Snoop was all right.

Mind was messing with me night and day until I was dying to find a way to shut down my mind completely. Just close my eyes and concentrate on something other than Uncle. Something other than this fuckin' penitentiary. Something like good food. Or good pussy. Anything to get my mind off death and dying and doom and gloom.

I was eating alone, thinking those kinds of thoughts, when this girl who knew I came from East Baltimore came up to me.

"You know that nigga you call Father?" she asked.

I didn't answer. I didn't wanna hear nothing about Father. Didn't wanna hear that he was dead. But she kept talking.

"He just got life."

"For what?"

"For everything. They came down on him hard. Got him on every last thing you can imagine. And they made the shit stick. He gonna be gone forever and a day."

They got Uncle.

Now they got Father.

Ain't gonna see Father again no more. He ain't dead, but he might as well be dead. Motherfucker's now a lifer.

These were my guys, my lifelines. How did my lifelines become my deathlines. How did all this happen?

News of Father coming after news of Uncle deepened the hole I was sliding down. Blues got bluer. Funk got funkier. Everything got uglier.

If someone had said, "Take this here pill. Won't hurt you none and you'll be dead in ten seconds," I might have swallowed it. Anything to get out of a world that was going against me.

I slept.

I sulked.

I let the darkness surround me until everyone was saying, "Snoop, you look half dead."

I was half dead and knew it wouldn't be long before the other half would crumble.

From one of the other cells I heard someone playing a song called "Sugar on the Floor."

That's what I felt like. All the sugar had spilled out of me and was on the floor. Nothing sweet was left. Hope was gone. Wasn't any way in the world for this condition to lift. It was heavier than anything I'd ever felt before. It was permanent. No doubt, it was taking me down.

And then one night when my eyes were half closed I looked through the window and saw a half moon. That's when it happened. Still don't understand it. All I can tell you is that it happened.

GRACE AFTER MIDNIGHT

I've never had a vision. Ain't never seen no angel. Never heard the voice of God say, "Hey, Snoop, do this or do that." Never heard the voice of God say nothing.

Back when I was a kid, Mama took me to her Holy Ghost Baptist Church. Pop had me over to where the Jehovah's Witnesses praised God. Far as I was concerned, it was all good. Wasn't like I got caught up in that shit, but I didn't see it doing no harm.

As time went on, and I hit the corners, Mama would try to get me back me in church, but I wasn't having it. Church didn't mean nothing to me then. Didn't have the time. Didn't have the interest.

Then when I got stuck in the city jail and later sent down to the Cut, I seen ladies who couldn't stop jumping for Jesus. They looked as crazy as the girls who were in there for murdering their boyfriends. Lots of time they *were* the girls who'd murdered their boyfriends. I stayed clear of them bitches.

Someone's always trying to convert your ass in jail. Someone's always throwing a Bible at you and getting you to see the light. Well, the only light I saw was the light coming out of that little window in my cell. I didn't see no magical light.

But something amazing did happen to me a month after Uncle got hit. I'm gonna try to describe it best as I can, but it ain't gonna be perfect. It can't be, 'cause I don't understand it.

I was sleeping. I was dreaming. I don't even remember the dream, but I do remember when I opened my eyes I thought I was still dreaming. I actually pinched myself real hard to make sure I wasn't dreaming. I wasn't.

I felt something. I felt a presence. Something was in that cell. Something was surrounding me. I felt like it was coming in me; and I felt like it was coming out of me. It was a sweet warm energy flowing all around me. It had me smiling. I had no reason to be smiling, but I was. I don't smile all that much, so for me to be smiling in the middle of the night for no goddamn reason is crazy. But this was crazy. This was more than a good feeling. This was something moving me and changing me and causing me to smile. This was saying to me, "It's all right. It's okay. Everything's cool. Everything's right." It wasn't saying that in words, but that was the feeling.

Then I felt Uncle's presence.

I ain't saying he came back from the grave. I didn't see nothing. But he was there with me. I know how it felt when Uncle came round, and, believe me, in the dead of night he had come round. Motherfucker was there.

He was there and carrying love with him. He was saying—least the feeling was saying—that love is something that's always there. It comes to you. You accept or you reject it. You accept it and it's yours. Reject it and it's gone. That's it.

You go up or you go down.

This middle-of-the-night feeling had me up. More up than I'd ever been in my life.

I was rejoicing for the feeling. I wanted to wake up every last bitch asleep at Grandma's House and tell 'em the good news.

Love's all around.

Love's come to town.

Love's in the Cut.

And that love wasn't nothing we had to buy or work for.

Was just there.

Free.

Beautiful.

———

Next morning I saw my godmother, Denise. I had to tell her about it. Denise is church people, and I knew she'd understand.

"That's grace," she said.

"What's grace?" I asked her.

"God's free love. It's yours. You get it 'cause he's giving it. He done paid the price for you."

"Grace," I repeated.

"Amazing grace," she added.

"It came after midnight," I said. "Grace after midnight."

HOME STRETCH

This business of counting days will drive you crazy.

I was still eighteen. My new good behavior was being noticed, but I knew I couldn't risk another negative move.

Now that I saw the light, I wanted to move into the light.

The light from that little window in my cell was shining brighter every day. Even if the day was gray, I'd see light inside the gray. The sky might be coal black, but I'd see light in a distant star.

If you look for light, you find it.

If you pray for hope, you get it.

I found light and I found hope.

When CO and I could manage our secret little meetings, she'd say, "Snoop, you a whole different person. I see you smiling."

"Uncle put that smile on my face," I said. "The only way I could have learned that lesson was through the fucked-up pain of his death. I saw what happened to him, my favorite guy in the world. Exact same thing was gonna happen to me if I didn't turn this shit around. I'd get out of here and start acting the fool all over again. Those negative vibes were all over me. You saw that."

"I've always seen something better than that in you," said CO. "I seen someone decent and good."

We'd hug, we'd kiss, and that'd be it. Better to live with sexual frustration than to get caught screwing a CO in the Cut.

Caution was the word.

I read me some good books, about Malcolm X, Dr. King, Muhammad Ali, and other black leaders.

I listened to some good music.

When I heard my girl Janet singing 'bout "I Get Lonely," I was wishing I could keep her company.

When Busta Rhymes was spittin' 'bout "Put Your Hands Where My Eyes Could See," I kept looking out that window in my cell and hoping the seasons would change faster.

Lil' Kim was blowin' up big. MC Lyte had out this jam called "Cold Rock a Party." Missy Elliott was rocking "The Rain." Juvenile, Jay Z, J-Lo, Ja Rule, JT Money, Ol' Dirty Bastard, Monifah and Monica and all kinds of shit was coming into the Cut. These sounds made me wanna get out of the Cut. But believe me, I wasn't planning no escape.

I believed in the grace business.

I knew I was blessed.

And knowing that gave me patience. Gave me fortitude. Gave me the wherewithal to grind it out, hour after hour, day after day.

I got me that GED.

Thank you, Jesus.

Got me those good behavior reports.

Thank you, Lord.

Got along with every bitch that came my way, even the ones looking to claw out my eyes.

Found a way to chill 'em out.

I'd explain it clearly. "Look here, bitch," I'd say, "I ain't looking to fuck up anyone and I ain't looking to get fucked up. So you best be moving on. You feeling me?"

They felt me. By then they knew I had a reputation that said, "Snoop is cool, but don't get on her wrong side."

My reputation for violence kept me peaceful.

"I'm changing my ways," I told CO.

Told my godmother, Denise, the same thing.

"No more temper tantrums," I said. "No more bullshit. I'm headed outta here and nothing can get in my way. Nothing except my own stupidity."

"You got that right," Denise agreed.

"I got lots of blessings," I said.

"You got God to thank," she told me.

"And I thank him," I assured her. "I thank him every goddamn day."

THE DAY OF DAYS

It'll happen. Time will pass.

You can look at your watch ten hours a day. You can watch the second hand go round and round until your eyes cross and you can't see straight no more. You can feel like time's slowing down. You can even feel like time's stopped, but, no, sir, it hasn't. It keeps moving.

An hour.

An afternoon.

An evening.

A day.

A week.

A month.

A year.

And then two years.

The routine's kicked in:

You sleeping all right. You eating all right. You getting in the rec room and shooting hoops all right. You squeezing in a little hidden time with your girlfriend. You studying up those books real good. Passing those tests. Being nice as you can be to the officers and the supervisors and the guards.

You getting by.

You letting that time pass and, believe it or not, you being cool about it all.

And then one day, you look up at the calendar and see that you're there. The day of days has arrived.

You getting your ass outta Grandma's House.

You kissing this fuckin' Cut good-bye.

Like the old folk say, "Free at last. Great God almighty, we're free at last!"

The day wasn't sunny. The day wasn't warm. There wasn't no rainbow in the sky and the birds weren't singing. Fact is, the weather was rainy and the sky was dark.

But I didn't give a shit.

A hurricane could be blowing on the outside, but I'd walk into it with a big ol' smile. To get outside the walls of the Cut, to step out of that joint into the cold air of freedom was all that mattered.

I had my little suitcase in my hand and was feeling lighter than air.

July 7, 2000.

Felicia Snoop Pearson, age twenty, was stepping out.

Felicia Snoop Pearson, former prisoner, was getting out early 'cause of good behavior and the work time she'd put together.

Felicia Snoop Pearson, former corner boy, former drug runner, former friend of every bad-ass nigga in East Baltimore, was taking her first breath of free air.

No bars in front of her; no bars behind her; no lockup at night; no checkup every hour; no one breathing down her neck.

The rain fell on my forehead. The rain felt great. There, by the curb, was Uncle's wife, waiting for me.

"He'd want me to do this," she said. "He'd be proud of you. Wherever you wanna go, Snoop, I'm happy to drive you."

"Take me to Mama's, please."

Mama was the first person I wanted to see. Hadn't seen the lady for six years, since I first went into city jail. Hadn't wanted her to see me locked up. Hadn't told her when I was getting out. Wanted to surprise her.

That drive to Baltimore was the best trip of my life. Everything looked beautiful. The passing cars. The billboards. The telephone poles. The Burger Kings. The motels. Even the white lines dividing the highway.

I kept closing my eyes and imagining I was still in the Cut. Then I opened them and smiled. I wasn't in the Cut. I was passing by a gas station, a school, a factory, a car wash, a playground.

On the radio Da Brat and Tyrese were singing "What 'Chu Like." I liked everything, everything I saw, everything I felt. I liked Destiny's Child. I liked DMX talkin' 'bout his "Party Up in Here."

At the same time, I wasn't looking for no party. Didn't

wanna drink and sure as shit didn't wanna drug. I was looking for Mama.

"Child," she said, as soon as I ran up the stairs, opened the door, and fell in her arms, "I sure wasn't looking for you. But now that I found you, I gotta praise the Lord. Gotta say, 'Thank you, Jesus.'"

She started crying, and I started crying along with her.

"Thank you, Lord," she kept whispering. "Thank you, sweet Lord."

She fixed me a big meal and called the relatives over to greet me. Everyone was cool. No one said a nasty word about where I'd been.

"We just happy to have you back" was the only word I heard.

Everyone congregated around the kitchen table while I devoured the best meal of my natural life. Baked chicken. Macaroni and cheese. Greens. Corn. Hot apple pie.

You couldn't tell me that life wasn't sweet.

One cousin said, "Tell us the worst thing that happened to you in there."

"Not being here" is all I said.

"She's prettier than ever," one of the aunts told Mama, nodding in my direction.

"Pretty on the outside and inside too," Mama said. "Minute I laid eyes on my baby, I saw the Lord had been dealing with her. She changed. God done put her in there for a reason."

I didn't disagree with Mama. On that day, I didn't disagree with anyone or anything. My mind was smiling as much as my mouth. I'd look out the front window of Mama's place, the windows where you see East Oliver, and remember the tiny window in my jail. How many times had I looked out the window?

Ten thousand? Ten million? Who knew?

When I looked out Mama's windows, I saw cars riding up and down the street. Kids playing. Dogs running. A taxicab. An ice cream truck.

I could just step out the house and buy an ice cream cone. No one would stop me. No one would look twice.

I did it. I bought the ice cream. Ate it. Sat on the stoop— that same stoop where I had first looked at the world, trying to understand the game—and just listened to the sound of my breathing.

Evening fell. The rain stopped. The city smelled fresh. I continued taking in the sights and sounds all around me. Sirens. Buses. Mothers calling in their children. The world going on. The world doing its thing.

I was back in the world.

I was going on.

But this time my thing would be different.

This time everything would be different.

LOVE, INSIDE AND OUT

There's inside love and outside love.

Love inside the Cut is strange love because you're locked up and nothing's normal. Your life ain't normal, your thoughts ain't normal, your dreams ain't normal. Your brain's scrambled by all the bricks and bars and the cold fact that you can't get out until they let you out. You're also surrounded by a whole lot of bitches who ain't never getting out. Their attitude about love will fuck you up.

You want love. You always want love, no matter where you at. At Grandma's House, when you find someone who seems sweet and nice, you grab on to her. Least I did. That was CO.

Inside the Cut, CO and I met in the secret corners to steal a kiss. That always felt good. She was cool. She talked about the day I'd be out of there, the day when we could be a couple, sleep in a bed together, and have us some real sex.

That day came soon after I got released. The sex was real. I liked all that. I thought CO and I had it going on.

We went to the movies like a regular couple. We saw silly movies like *Big Momma's House* and laughed our asses off. We saw scary movies like *Scream 3* and action movies like *Mission: Impossible II*. Having a date, ordering a Coke and a box of buttered popcorn, holding hands, and sleeping all night with a lady I loved—these were good things.

But I soon learned that love outside the Cut is different than love inside the joint.

"Where were you yesterday?" CO asked.

"Talking to my parole officer," I said.

"What about?"

"About getting me a job. You know, they got that re-entry program. I been trained real good to fill out applications. They taught me how to make a good impression during interviews."

"Is your parole officer that tall woman with the big tits?" CO asked.

"I'm an ass man," I reminded her.

"She likes girls, don't she?"

"She married with two kids."

"What difference does that make?"

"I'm just another case to her," I said.

"I thought you said she likes you."

"She does. But not the way you worried about."

"I ain't worried," said CO.

"You sounding worried."

"I just don't see how it could take all day to meet with your parole officer."

"Didn't say it took all day."

"Then what'd you do the rest of the day?" CO wanted to know.

"Helped Mama in the kitchen."

"You didn't go out?" she asked.

"I did go out."

"Where to?"

"The store."

"And then what'd you do?"

"Picked up a bitch with a big butt and fucked her brains out all afternoon."

"You don't need to be sarcastic," said CO.

"But that's what you worried about, ain't it? You think I'm fucking someone behind your back. Well, I ain't. I'm the loyal type."

"I still wanna know where—"

"I ain't answering no more questions," I snapped. "You can believe whatever you wanna believe."

Next day CO called and apologized. "There's a movie that's supposed to be funny," she said, "called *Miss Congeniality*. Let's go see it."

I said fine.

We went to a gay bar afterward. CO was anything but Miss Congeniality.

"I don't like the way that bitch over there is looking at you," she said.

I said, "Ain't shit I can do about it."

"You don't got to look back at her."

"I wasn't looking till you mentioned her."

"Let's get out of here," said CO.

"We just got here."

"If you stay, you're staying alone."

"I'm staying," I said.

"'Cause you wanna pick up on that bitch, right?"

"'Cause I wanna finish my drink."

"I got drinks at my place."

"Then why the hell did we come to a bar?"

"It was your idea," she said. "You wanted to check out the merchandise."

"Fuck you," I said.

"You chasing me off. Is that it?"

"I'm telling your bossy ass that I'm gonna sit here and finish my drink—that's what I'm doing."

"And I'm telling you it's time we got outta here."

That's when I turned my back on CO.

"If I walk out that door now," she threatened, "you're never seeing me again."

I didn't say nothing.

"All those years you were in Grandma's House," she went on, "all that time we spent together—you willing to throw it away?"

Still didn't say nothing.

"I'm telling you, Snoop, I'm demanding you leave with me right now."

She put her hand on my shoulder.

I knocked her hand away.

No overbearing bitch was gonna put me in prison. I'd just got outta prison. That prison was made of concrete. CO's prison was made of jealousy. Both prisons would make me miserable.

It was a tough lesson, but at least I was learning it early on: Love inside the Cut one's thing; outside it's another.

BOYS DON'T CRY

Breaking up with CO didn't put me in a bad mood. Being free to walk the streets and look for a job—man, that was enough to keep me happy 24/7.

I was gung-ho to follow up on this re-entry program and do myself proud. Living back at Mama's house, I was doing everything right.

I'd turned over a new leaf and wanted to stay on the straight and narrow.

I felt the blessing. I felt the grace.

And even though I was sorry the thing between me and CO didn't work out, I stayed away because I wasn't interested in hooking up with someone ruled by jealousy. Life is too short for that shit.

I didn't go running into another relationship. That ain't me. I've never been promiscuous. Never been known to run around with two different girls at once. Truth is, I've had only a couple of serious relationships. I don't need to be with a woman on a date to have a good time.

Lots of time I go out by myself. I like seeing movies alone.

Not long after I got out of the Cut, I went to see Hillary Swank in *Boys Don't Cry*. I'd heard it was about a girl who pretended to be a boy. People said it was a great movie. I wanted to check it out.

I sat in that dark theater, and I couldn't believe my eyes. Couldn't believe how much I loved the story and loved the movie.

I identified with the girl called Brandon who wanted to be a boy.

I felt that her pain was my pain, her dilemma my dilemma, her heart my heart. She was sweet and she was good. Wasn't looking to hurt no one. She was just being who she was. She was good people. I was rooting for her to get by.

I was deep into the love story. I knew that a girl who feels like a boy can fall in love with a girl. And I know that a girl can love a girl who dresses and acts like a boy. I been there. I done that. That shit's real.

The whole movie was real. Hillary Swank chewed it up. As an actress, she had balls, just like the Brandon girl she was playing had balls. That whole movie had balls to show what it was showing. It had balls 'cause it made you love the Brandon girl. Didn't judge her. Didn't make it like she was sick or wrong. The movie understood. The movie loved her. And you had to love the movie.

Well, I did. I was rooting for Brandon. I forgot, at least for a minute, that it was a real story that had a real ending. I was rooting for a happy ending. Come on, Brandon. You can do it. You can act like a boy, love on a girl, and have a happy life. You can get by. You can survive all the ignorance and hate that the world puts on gays. You get what you want and come out a winner. In the end, good triumphs over bad. Love wins all. Brandon's gonna get through this thing. Brandon's gonna survive. Gotta survive 'cause her heart is right and she ain't hurt a fly and there's no reason to hurt her.

And then it happens.

They rape her. And then they came in there with all the guns and stuff. And they murder her.

Boys don't cry, but I was crying. If you had a goddamn heart, you had to be crying. And then I got mad. Real fuckin' mad. And then I got to thinking:

If a big boy tried to rape me like that, I wouldn't fight back because, one by one, a big boy will beat up a smaller female. Ain't shit you can do. But afterward I'd come back. I'd come back when he thought everything was good. I'd come when he was sleeping. I'd come back and cut off his balls with a knife, slice off his dick, shove it up his butt and blow his fuckin' brains out with a gun.

That's what I'd do to the motherfucker who messed up Brandon.

That's what I'd like to do all the motherfuckers who make fun of gay people by scaring 'em and hurting 'em and torturing 'em and humiliating 'em and treating 'em like we dirt.

Boys Don't Cry broke my heart and enraged my mind that there's still all these assholes out there who got nothing better to do than mess up people different from them. Why? What's the point? What they trying to prove?

Ain't we all supposed to be children of God?

Ain't he supposed to love us the way we are?

Ain't this grace business about not having to do nothing to get God's love? He already loves you. He can't do nothing *but* love you.

He don't love just white or black or gay or straight. He don't say this church is wrong and that church is right.

He's just loving.

The guys who killed Brandon were a long way from feeling that love.

All they was feeling was blind hate.

Like Uncle say, you go up or you go down.

UP

Got that *Boys Don't Cry* movie outta my head. Got CO outta my head, too. I got plans to make, a job to get, a life to live.

I'm gonna jump into this re-entry program my parole officer's been helping me with. Re-enter the city. Re-enter society. Re-enter the workforce. Become a useful citizen. Use the skills I learned in the Cut. Go straight. Stay straight. Stay connected to hardworking people doing good. Avoid the assholes and hang with the achievers.

Got me a plan.

Got me new energy.

Good energy.

Clear-eyed clearheaded energy.

Got me this training that says, "When you fill out an application, and if it asks whether you've been to jail, leave it blank. Then during the interview, when and if the question comes up, explain how you did your time, earned your

GED, and are 100 percent rehabilitated. That way you have a chance to get a job. But if you indicate on that application that you've been to jail, that might prevent you from getting the interview."

I was ready, set, go.

The training had me thinking positive. I was clean. I was smiling. I was talking correctly and displaying good manners. When I went to the employment agency, I was on my Sunday best behavior.

Man looked at me and said, "You look like a strong girl."

"I am, sir."

"Looks like you wouldn't mind manual labor."

"Not at all, sir."

"Working in a factory bother you?"

"Working in a factory sounds good."

"You sure got a positive attitude."

"Gotta be positive, sir. Positive is what gets us through."

"Well, you're getting through to me," he said. "I see an opening at a car plant. They need a worker on the line where they make those bumpers. You interested?"

"Very interested, sir."

"When you can start?"

"The second I leave here."

He laughed. "You're not making bumpers in those nice clothes, are you?"

"I'll pick me up some overalls on the way, sir."

"You can show up tomorrow morning. I'll call the foreman now. He'll be happy to have someone this eager to work."

"And I'll be happy to help him any way I can, sir."

That was it!

I walked out of that agency smiling from ear to ear. First interview, and *swish! I score!* Nothing but net.

I had a job. I was on my way.

Went home and told Mama, who, of course, gave the glory to God. That was okay with me. Maybe it was God. Maybe it's always God.

Well, with God's light finally shining down on me, I walked past the corner where the boys were dealing dope and didn't give those niggas a second glance. My pay might be meager and my hours long, but the work was legit and the job was real. You had to be responsible to work this gig. And the company had to have some faith in me to put me in the factory.

I had followed the training course, and the training course was working. I didn't indicate I'd been to jail on the application, and, to my happy surprise, the guy never brought it up. If he had, I was ready with an answer—I'd paid my debt to society, I'd done my time and come out a better person. But the question never came up. He was a good guy. He saw that I was all about wanting a good job, and he gave me a break.

That night I sat in the bathtub listening to my Mary J. jams. I wanted to relax before the big day. I didn't want to go out and celebrate. Didn't wanna party because I was seeing that work would be my party. Work would be where I could find the real joy in my life. Work—honest work—is what I'd always missed. Having a boss. Being responsible to the boss. Learning quickly and getting ahead. I'd always bucked the system, but now I wanted the system. Wanted it to work for me. Would *make it* work for me.

Slept a dreamless sleep.

Got up early.

Felt refreshed.

Mama made oatmeal, fresh-squeezed orange juice, toast, and jam.

Put on a clean new pair of overalls. Fixed myself a couple of sandwiches for lunch.

Joined the other workers of the world as we waited at the bus stop.

I felt regular.

Felt good.

Caught the bus.

Got off at the plant.

Went through doors, walking proud, looking for my foreman.

"Hello, new world," I said to myself. "I'm ready."

THE LINE

I'd been in police lineups, but I'd never worked an assembly line.

Tell you the truth, I liked the assembly line. Had a rhythm, a definite groove. I liked the movement, liked seeing those auto parts dancing down the belt. It was sort of exciting.

I thought of Pop, the man who had me working next to him all during my childhood. Pop had taught me the value of hard work. He had shown me that I have a knack for making things and fixing things. Pop had given me the confidence that I was showing my foreman.

Foreman was impressed. He saw I was willing and capable of doing anything the men could do. He respected me.

I caught on quick. I could handle the speed of the assembly line in no time. I could handle placing the right parts in the right places. I could handle some of the guys looking at me like they wanted to say, "What's this bitch doing here?"

After a day or two, I even made friends with some of the guys. Once they saw I could stand with them toe to toe, they gave me props.

I got to work early. Worked my ass off. Sometimes I didn't even bother taking the breaks so I could get more work done.

I was on fire.

I wanted to shine.

I wanted to show everyone that I could hack it, I could do whatever they gave me to do.

At night, I went home tired, but it was a good tired. I'd go to sleep early and wake up at the crack of dawn, ready to go again.

"You sure are the eager beaver," said Mama.

"I'm working on a promotion," I said after I'd been there a short while. "Foreman says if I keep going the way I'm going, he could bump me up to an assembly line that pays a little more."

"Just keep at it, baby," Mama encouraged me. "I sure am proud of you."

I was proud of myself.

The shit had sure-enough turned around.

The way a good rap has a good flow, well, my work life had a flow. I was making bumpers and I was making friends. I was seeing how the straight life was the good life. When you get off from eight hours of solid manual labor, when you don't try to cut corners and give it your best, you feel good about yourself.

I was feeling great about myself.

"Snoop," said the foreman one afternoon, "would you step into my office for a minute."

"Yes, sir," I said.

Here's that promotion, I thought.

"Snoop," he said, "I gotta let you go."

"What!"

"Got no choice."

"I thought I was working out."

"You were working out great."

"Then what's wrong?"

"Your jail record. They told me you served long time down in the pen."

"I did," I said, "but I never said I didn't. It never came up in the interviews."

"Well, it's come up now."

"And you can't say nothing for me?"

"I said a lot of things for you, Snoop, but my boss over-ruled. He said you're dealing with sharp metal down here, and with your record, that's dangerous."

"That's bullshit. I ain't hurting nobody. I ain't even arguing with nobody. You seen me arguing?"

"Not once, but, like I said, Snoop, I don't got the final say."

"There ain't no way to appeal this?"

"'Fraid not. They say you gotta clear outta here."

"Today?"

"You'll get paid for today, but I've been told to escort you out."

"Like I'm a criminal," I said, "like I done something terrible here on the job."

"I don't like it any more than you do, but that's the way it is. All I can do is wish you luck."

"I'll need it."

IF AT FIRST YOU DON'T SUCCEED . . .

. . . try and try again.

That's what Pop always said when we were making stuff together.

If I hammered a nail crooked or patched the roof wrong, Pop would say, "Getting it right takes time."

Mama reminded me of that when I got home from being fired.

"Sure, you're discouraged," she said. "You can't help but be. But hang in there. You did good at that job. You'll do better on the next."

Gotta confess that it took me a week or so to get my spirits back up. I had a big resentment to shake off. Back in the Cut, they had told me if I followed this program and took their advice, I'd work.

Well, I took their advice and got canned.

Getting fired makes you feel like shit. And especially after you break your ass to do a good job. Getting fired unfairly makes you mad.

But what could I do with my anger?

Wasn't no one's fault. If the assholes who run this car plant wouldn't give me a break, I'd find someone who could. I'd keep my attitude positive. I'd think about the things that Uncle told me. I'd think about all the prayers that Mama and my godmother Denise said for me.

I'd go back out there and find another job.

"Glad you're not discouraged," the guy at the employment agency said to me.

"Not discouraged," I told him, "just determined. Determined to get something and keep it."

At first he didn't have anything, but I kept going back.

A week passed. Then two.

Finally, when I went the third time, he was smiling.

"Found something for you, Snoop," he said.

"I knew you would," I said. "I'm about to luck up."

LUCKED UP OR FUCKED UP?

Back at Grandma's House, they called it Job Readiness. They made a big deal of it. I took the shit seriously and wound up working at the car plant. After I got jacked up at the car plant, it took a little minute to clean up my attitude.

But I did.

I was back on the positive tip. I was ready to take this job the employment agency was offering at some book warehouse.

"What do I have to do?" I asked the guy.

"Haul boxes. Heavy ones. That bother you?"

"Fuck no."

First day of the gig, Mama fixed me another big breakfast. She prayed on me. She said, "Lord, thank you for blessing this child with your grace. Thank you for touching her heart with your love."

I caught the bus. I was back in the workforce. I'd gotten out of the Cut in July. Now it was September. The weather was still warm, the world still looking good to me. I couldn't help but remember back to how it was inside Grandma's House. Those bars, those bricks, those endless days, endless weeks, endless months and years.

Hell, I was grateful to be sitting on a bus, a free woman with a new job.

Foreman was a white cat. Nice enough. He presumed I was strong or I wouldn't be there—and he was right. I lifted the heaviest boxes they had. I hauled the shit all day long until one guy looked at me and said, "Girl, you stronger than two of us." I just nodded.

I got through the first day fine.

That night I went out to Buns, a club up on Lexington and Green. It was a mixed club, gay men and women, and since I got out of jail I had noticed how many more gay women were out of the closet. I had had me a couple of little romances, but nothing permanent. I wasn't interested in permanent. I was interested in celebrating the fact that I got another job. I was sipping on wine when a gal came up to me, real aggressivelike, and started talking. I don't like aggressive. I ignored her, but she got loud and testy. I could see she might be trouble. When she started cussing me, I ignored her. I'd learned my lesson about getting into it with crazy bitches. I moved on. Went home and went to sleep. Tomorrow's another day.

Tomorrow brought another challenge. Cat at work came up to me and said, "What's a skanky bull dyke doing working at a place like this?"

I just looked at the motherfucker. My eyes said, *Fuck with me and I'll cut your nuts off,* but my mouth didn't say shit. I kept doing what I was doing.

That didn't satisfy him.

"I hate dykes," he said. "Women ain't got no business eating pussy."

I kept on loading.

He kept on provoking, saying all sorts of raunchy shit.

I wanted to go upside his side so bad I could hardly contain myself. But I did. I pretended the asshole wasn't even there.

Finally, when he shoved me real hard, I was about to lose it and knee him in the balls. That's when God or good luck stepped in. The foreman was walking by, heard what the guy was saying, and fired his ass, right then and there.

Things were changing for me. The timing was good.

The job was good. I liked working in the warehouse more than the factory. Wasn't as loud. No sharp parts to cut your hands. Plus, other than the asshole who'd been dogging me, nicer people. Even made a couple of friends.

Life was finally taking a good turn. The days were going by. The nights were calm. The weekends could be fun, especially if I got lucky on Saturday—all girls' night—at Buns. I was staying out of trouble. And even saving some money.

Was completing my second month at the warehouse. Feeling confident. Finally settling into a routine that seemed to make sense. The guys were always complaining about sore backs and sore arms from all that lifting, but I was fine. I could do this thing.

Arrived on a Monday morning.

As usual, I was the first one there. Eager to get started. Went to the little locker where I stashed my lunch, opened it, and saw an envelope. Inside was a slip that said my services were no longer required.

Took the slip and went to the foreman.

"Why?" I asked.

"Your jail record."

I said what I said to the last foreman. I hadn't been asked about jail. If I had been, I would have told the truth, but it never came up.

This cat was cold.

"Tough shit," he said. "You're out."

I kept trying to explain.

He cut me off and said, "We don't want ex-cons here."

This was the same guy who'd been telling how well I'd been working out, the same guy who saw I could outlift almost every fuckin' man in the warehouse. I hadn't missed a day, hadn't gotten into a single argument, much less a fight. I was the model goddamn worker.

"Can I just say—" I began to argue.

"You can't say shit."

I thought about ending this job by slugging the foreman. I came awfully close, but I didn't.

What was the point?

Here all this time I thought I had lucked up, but I was really fucked up.

In my head, I was fucked up bad.

CAR WASH

There's a funny movie they made way back in the day called *Car Wash*. I watched it on TV a couple of times. Richard Pryor plays a hustling preacher. The jams are poppin' and the story's real good.

My story at the car wash ain't real good.

I took the gig to get my parole office off my back. After the first two fuckups, I was bummed out. I did what I was told to do and wound up getting screwed. I not only worked, I worked my ass off. I worked until I was sore from my head to my toe. Every muscle ached. Every good feeling I'd had went bad. Positive turned to negative. Sunshine turned to shit. All my eagerness, all my go-for-it energy, all my it's-gonna-turn-out-good energy turned rotten. I was sugar on the floor.

But I also figured I needed to do what I needed to do. Was a car wash any worse than slapping bumpers on cars or lugging around boxes of books? Besides, everyone in the movie *Car Wash* seemed to be having fun.

It was the end of summer. The last blast of heat was pushing through Baltimore. The radio was blasting Jay Z "Big Pimpin'."

The line never stopped. Motors kept churning. Engines kept burning. Put me on the wash line. Slap on the soap. Soap up the windows. Soap up the hood. Soap up the doors and the fenders. Soap up the Corvette, soap up the Jag and the Lexus. Listen to the rich bitch scream that we ain't using enough soap. Think about soaping up her big mouth. Think about the lunch break. Hear the bossman screaming, "Wash cars, hurry up, wash those fuckin' cars."

Do it all day Monday. Do it Tuesday and Wednesday and Thursday and Friday. Work a ten-hour shift on Saturday. Sleep late Sunday and when you wake up remember that all your fuckin' dreams were about washing cars. You can't stop washing cars.

I wanna stop washing cars. I wanna do something better with my life. I take off a day to go out on other interviews—office jobs, factory jobs, jobs at the mall, jobs in hotels. But every interview comes down to asking me about my past. In every interview I tell the truth. And in every interview I'm told they ain't interested. See ya later. Don't slam the door behind you. Have a nice day.

So it's back to soaping up cars. The tricked-out pickup trucks. The big-ass Escalades. The Ferraris that cost more than twice as much as my mama's house. Sometimes I think of getting behind the wheel of one of those motherfuckers and driving off. Up to D.C., up to New York City, up to Canada until no one can find me and the goddamn car is mine. Stupid fantasies. Just soap up the cars. Soap up my life. Soap up my brain. Wash the bad thoughts away. Thoughts of going back to the block. Thoughts of doing what it seems I'm supposed to do—work the corners.

You don't need no interview to work the corners. No one asks you questions and looks into your past. You don't gotta worry about being accepted. You don't gotta negotiate no salary. It's every nigga for himself. It's survival of the fuckin' fittest. That's what I'm fit for. That's what I'm born for. That's who I am.

But I think of Uncle, and I think of Mama, I think of Denise and all the good people in my life and I go back to soaping up the cars. It's ten in the morning. It's two in the afternoon. It's almost time to get off.

I smell of soap.

"You ain't soaping like you mean it," says the bossman as I walk out the door.

"Excuse me?" I say. *What the fuck does that mean?*

"You doing a lame-ass job."

"This *is* a lame-ass job," I tell him.

"You missing spots."

"Bullshit," I say.

"And the guys don't like working with no bull dyke."

I snap. "You know what? You and the other guys can go fuck yourselves in the ass. Fuck you, fuck the other guys, fuck this car wash, and fuck every motherfuckin' car-drivin' asshole who comes in here. I'm out."

LIFE AIN'T NO MOVIE

Life ain't no comedy. Ain't no folks singing songs on the car wash line. Ain't no cute jokes and ain't no happy ending.

That's how I was thinking when I told the car wash cat to fuck himself. I was fed up. Fed up with knocking my head against the wall. Fed up with niggas' fucked-up attitudes. Fed up with name-calling. This so-called straight world out here was no world I could relate to. It was a world I had to leave. I'd tried it and I'd fuckin' failed. So it was good-bye to bad garbage. I was going back to the only world where I'd ever done any good, the world where bad was good and where I was super-bad.

My rep was already established on the street. My shit was already standing. My shit was marked in stone.

I paid my dues. I had sat my little ass down in the Cut for a minute.

Now the minute was up.

Now I said, "Fuck everything else."

I was tired of struggling.

I could have talked to Mama, but I didn't.

I could have talked to my godmother, Denise, but I didn't.

Could have found a cool counselor or some righteous preacher, but fuck the counselor and fuck the preacher. I was tired of this fucked-up do-goody attitude. I was tired of being someone I would never be.

Back to the dog-eat-dog world.

Back to get it when you can.

Back to the goddamn block.

Ain't gonna fight with no one. Just bust a move and jump outta sight. Move outta Mama's house. Move in with a girlfriend. She's pretty cool. She lets me runs things. She knows I'm the man in the relationship. She don't bug me about where I'm going and how I'm making a dollar.

I got me five hundred dollars saved.

Take that five hundred, buy me a half ounce of coke, and work off that.

That's it.

That's the start.

Put that Mickey Mouse go-straight shit out of my head.

Think like I used to think.

Think ahead.

Start dealing with this coke and move up to heroin. More money in heroin.

Got one thought and one thought only:

Start slow, stay cool, but wind up the biggest drug dealer in East Baltimore.

This time fuckin' go for it.

I know the game.

Now I'm playing to win.

DICKHEAD

I called him a dickhead 'cause he *was* a dickhead. I called him a fuckin' prick cause he hated my ass so bad he bent the rules. He wanted the satisfaction of locking me up—and he did.

I was out there on the corner. Since the car wash bust, I had only been out there for a hot second. Got my shit together. Got me a couple of corner boys to watch for the cops. And got me a couple of hitters who would run the drugs to the customers in the cars. I knew what I was doing.

But this particular cop had attitude flying out his ass. Every time I was ready to open shop in the morning, he'd cruise by and talk much shit.

"Gonna get your ass, nigga," he'd sneer.

I wouldn't say nothing back. Wouldn't even look at the motherfucker. Naturally that made him angrier. He wanted some kind of reaction. I just turned my back. When he was gone, I went about doing my business.

It was like that for a while.

Then one morning he came by all worked up.

"This is it," he said. "Your time's up."

I just smiled, shrugged, and walked on.

Half hour later the dickhead's back. He runs his car up on the curb and pins me against the building, charges out, and cuffs me. Meanwhile, his partner comes out the alley with ten pills of ready-rock.

"These yours?" asks Dickhead.

"Hell, no," I say.

"I'm sayin' they are."

"I'm sayin' you're full of shit. You just puttin' this shit on me."

He smiled and said, "I told you I'd get you."

We go downtown. I know this is a setup. I know I'm getting out of this.

I'm feeling okay until the judge looks at my record, sighs, then closes his eyes, and then slaps on a seventy-five-thousand-dollar bail.

That means to stay free I gotta cough up three stacks (three thousand dollars) for the bail.

Here comes the lawyer talkin' 'bout another two and a half stacks.

Here comes all that pretrial stuff.

Here comes all the accusations, all the phony charges.

Here comes the pressure.

Here comes the knowledge that if this shit goes against me, my ass is back in the Cut for fifteen years.

Here comes the report saying I had drugs stashed in the alley.

But here comes my lawyer showing that if I was selling drugs I wouldn't stash them that far away. That's not how we do. He makes this logical and beautiful argument about how the case makes no sense. He chews up their shit and spits it back in their face.

Case dismissed.

I'm off. I'm out.

But, in addition to the five and a half stacks I had to pay for bail and lawyers, I'm out another fifteen stacks because my stash got hit while all this legal crap was coming down.

Dickhead costs me over twenty stacks.

But I'm cool.

Or am I?

"I'LL BUST YOU WITH THIS BRICK!"

That's what I'm screaming at the bitch. And I mean it. I'm ready to go upside her head.

She's a relative of Mama's. I call her Aunt, but right now I'm calling her evil 'cause she's calling me a "little dyke-ass bitch." She's saying, "Mama ain't even your real mama. You don't deserve no real mama. You born in garbage and you *is* garbage."

I'm walking down the street, on my way pick up Chinese food for Mama, while she's slinging these insults at me. She's screaming 'cause I put her out of Mama's house. I put her out the house 'cause she's high all the time. High as a mother-fucker and making Mama crazy. I put her out the house to protect Mama.

Now she's coming after me. And she done brought the police with her. She lied and told the police that Mama's house is *her* house. Well, it ain't. She don't got no house, which is why she's living off Mama.

She keeps yelling at me. I'm trying to walk away but the words keep flying and the cop wants to talk to me.

She prods the cops. She tells them, "Ask this dyke bull how many other dyke bulls she fucked down in prison. They let her out by mistake. She should be back there with all them other bull dykes."

The cop starts asking me questions, but this evil bitch keeps on screaming until I pick up the cinder block and say, "I'm gonna kill this bitch! Gonna kill her right now."

"You ain't killing no one," says the cop.

That's when they straight lock me up and hustle me downtown.

Just what I need.

Another charge against me. Another night in jail. Another reason for the judge to send me back to the Cut.

Another long hard night. Another jail cell with another window with another full moon reminding me of all the moons I saw from the little window at Grandma's House.

In the morning I'm scheduled to go before the judge where charges will be pressed.

I got a lot on my mind.

Takes a long time to fall asleep.

When I do, I dream of my dead mother. She's alive in the dream and we're back together. We're walking down the street, about to go in a pawn shop where she's going to buy me a nine-millimeter to protect myself, when someone comes up from behind her and shoots her dead in the head. I wake up and remember I'm back in jail.

God knows what'll happen to me.

Does God even care?

Do I even care?

It'll be what it'll be.

But true to form, this bitch is too high to show up in court. There's no one to press charges.

I'm free.

Another chance.

I dodge another bullet.

I could see this is as an opportunity to mend my ways and go straight. But I've been through that straight shit before.

It don't work.

Besides, my business is going good. My shops are thriving.

My corner is hot.

COP SAYS, "CRACK YOUR ASS CHEEKS SO I CAN LOOK UP IN THERE."

That's what the cops say when they suspect you holding. Things are changing. Getting tighter, stricter, meaner. Lean times means you gotta get smarter. Ain't like back in the day when the shit was loose. Game's getting rougher.

But I'm playing. I'm schooling my boys. I'm telling them, "Be cool. Be smart. Not only will these motherfuckers crack your ass and look up your hole, they'll look up under your balls to see if you hiding rock there. So learn the hood, know who lives here and who don't, study every goddamn car cruising through, pay attention, niggas, and don't make no stupid mistakes."

My niggas had to be steely, steady, and ready to step. They had to have their heads on straight. If they were too nervous, they'd scatter when they didn't need to. If they were too spacey, they'd stay when it was time to scatter.

I trained 'em. I said, "Watch my eyes. Watch my eyes watching the street. I don't give out no expressions. My eyes ain't saying that I'm happy or sad or tired or wired. My eyes are dead set on the street. I can tell you exactly how many people passed by in the last thirty minutes, and I can tell you the color of their clothes. Damn near tell you the color of their eyes. You gotta be a hawk, niggas. You gotta be a goddamn hawk to get through this mess out here."

I was flying high. I was flying low. I was flying the right speed and the right distance. I was flying under the radar. Once in a while they might nab me for loitering, but I was in and out in a hot minute. Nothing was sticking on me. Nothing holding me back.

Broke up with that old girlfriend and found me another. Thought it might be serious but it turned out she was cheating. Girl she was cheating with was a bitch who looked like the Predator. I ain't kidding. But it was no big deal. What I thought was real romance wasn't real at all.

Cool.

I could find a girlfriend when I wanted one.

Besides, what I really wanted was to keep my shops poppin'.

I wanted to get bigger at the game.

That was my fate, my life, my only way of surviving.

I'd been in and I'd been out. Up and down. And even sideways. I knew which way was right for me.

Don't argue with me.

Don't tell me any different.

Don't give me no attitude.

If you wanna work for me, study the streets.

Maybe I'll give you a corner. Maybe I'll keep you around, look around to see how you do under fire.

You get one chance, but not two. If you fuck up the first time, that second chance could land me back at Grandma's House.

Ain't going back.

Going forward.

Don't get in my way.

"NO, NIGGA. I HIT THE BLOCK."

It was a Sunday night. Not much happening. Just hanging with a friend.

We were at a bar called Club One. Straight bar. Everything was cool.

I noticed this guy mad-dogging at me. He looked like a crime-type dude, so I looked the other way. But he kept staring.

"Who is that motherfucker?" I asked my friend.

"Michael K. Williams. He plays the gay gangsta on *The Wire*.

"What's *The Wire?*" I wanted to know.

My friend told me it was a TV show about Baltimore.

A little later Michael came over asked me, "You act or rap?"

"No, nigga," I said. "I hit the block."

"Well, come down to the set of *The Wire*. There some folks you should meet."

Next day I asked people I knew who watched the show what it was all about.

"People like you," they said.

"What does that mean?" I asked.

"Real people."

I wasn't thinking all that much about it, but figured I didn't have anything to lose.

So I went down to the show. When I got there, with all the trailers and shit, it didn't look like much to me.

"Please wait," they said.

"Wait for what?" I asked.

"Your screen test."

Well, I didn't know nothing about no screen test.

"What *is* a screen test?" I asked.

"We'll show you in a minute."

It was more than a minute. It was a long goddamn time. I was sitting in there, doing nothing but making calls to make sure my shops were running smooth.

Two hours later, I'd had it. I was about to get up and leave—fuck this shit—when they said they was ready.

Took me in a room, sat me down, and said, "You don't need to speak. Just look in the camera."

I looked in the camera for a couple of minutes.

I got paid $150.

"That's it?" I asked.

"That's it," they said.

"What's next?"

"We'll call you."

They did. They actually called the next day wanting another screen test. They said they'd pay another $150.

But I was thinking that's bullshit.

While I was getting $150 for a screen test I could be making many stacks on the block. In my business, time is money.

But on second thought, everyone thinks about being on TV, and I was no different. I started watching the show. *The Wire* had street characters running around every episode. I related. I liked the show. It was real.

"Okay," I said. "I'll take another test."

Second test happened. And a third.

Then someone came up and said, "You're a natural. We want you on the show."

I was a little shocked.

I didn't really believe it.

"No acting lessons?" I asked.

"No acting lessons," they said. "The directors will help you out."

I was feeling weird. I was feeling happy but I was also feeling like I was dreaming. They actually wanted to put me on TV.

"How 'bout my look?" I asked.

"We like your look," they said.

"I don't need to change it?"

"We don't want you to change it."

"How 'bout the way I talk?" I talk with this heavy Baltimore accent.

"We like the way you talk."

"It's all good?" I asked.

"All good," they said.

It's too good, I thought to myself. *My life don't work this way. It's too fuckin' good.*

FLIPPING THE SCRIPT

I knew *The Wire* was an HBO show for American TV, but I didn't know it was poppin' all over the world.

I didn't know, at the end of the third season of the series, when I started appearing, that I'd be so relaxed around the camera.

I had no idea that I'd take to it the way I did.

Strange, but I didn't look at it like acting.

It was being.

I just had to be.

On the show I had to be me: someone who hits the block.

They wanted me to keep my walk and my talk and even my name. They wanted me to be Snoop.

The other thing was this: Whenever and wherever we shot, I found myself in the middle of a family that loved me. All the actors, writers, and producers treated me like a long-lost daughter or sister or friend.

So there I was, doing what I'd always done: being a thug, only being a thug in front of the cameras.

What kind of crazy shit is that?

Suddenly I'm being recognized in restaurants. I'm being asked to act in other movies.

Real is pretend, and pretend is real.

Snoop is real-life me and Snoop is a pretend-life character on TV.

The script is flipped.

I wake up in the morning, get dressed, leave my work on the block to walk into a world about make-believe work on the block.

But because I ain't that sure the make-believe work is real, I keep my real-life work. My shops stay open.

"How long can you do that, Snoop?" asks my godmother, Denise. "How long can you keep selling dope?"

So Denise starts convicting me, and my conscience starts convicting me. My brain's spinning around and I'm getting confused all over again, just like when I was down in the Cut and learned that Uncle had been killed.

Back then I'd decided to go straight.

I'd seen the light.

But then when I got out and kept getting canned from straight jobs, the light went out.

I was drawn back into the darkness because the darkness was where I belonged. I was sure that the light was for others, not for me. I'd live and die in darkness. I'd even get rich in darkness. Darkness was all I knew. Darkness was my reality.

Now here comes all this *Wire* business.

TV cats talking about, "We want real people on this show. We want to show your reality."

But by showing my reality, these motherfuckers are changing my reality.

The shit's confusing.

By showing who I really am, they're changing who I really am.

I'm seeing that light again.

I'm feeling that love.

I'm thinking about closing down my shops. I'm thinking about not hitting the block anymore.

If I keep hitting the block, I'll fuck up this acting business. I'll fuck up everything. Getting other niggas killed or locked up. I'll get sent back to jail or I'll be killed.

Ain't no way around it.

The only way to leave my fucked-up reality is to throw myself into the pretend version of my fucked-up reality.

If I move toward the light—the light of the cameras, the light of the beautiful people who are running *The Wire* and acting on *The Wire*—then I escape the darkness.

The Wire is throwing light on that darkness.

That's what the show's about.

That's what I'm about.

My new life.

My new direction.

New light.

New hope.

New everything.

NEW SNOOP

New Snoop—the Snoop that's finally closed down her shops—is trying to make sense of this scene about a nail gun.

But the scene don't make sense and New Snoop's feeling stupid.

That's how it went in the beginning. I'd get some scripts that didn't make sense to me. I had trouble with the script supervisor, the gal who helps you with your lines. She was getting on my nerves and it took me a while to get used to her. Fact is, I never forgot my lines. I memorized them cold and never missed a beat.

I was still a little uneasy, though. Other than down at the courthouse, I'd never been around so many white people. It was a new experience. I didn't know what half of them did. I didn't understand how film works. I was nervous.

The thing about me, though—the thing I learned from

the streets—is not to show it. Keep my cool. Make it seem like I got my shit together.

That's what Snoop the Character is all about. And that's what Snoop the Actor has to be about too.

So I followed the directions I was given. I bonded with a couple of the actors. Michael K. Williams plays Omar. He's the one who got me through the door. Jamie Hector plays Marlo, the gangsta who hires me to kill niggas. Sometimes Omar, Hector, and I would hang out after the show. Sometimes they'd give me little pieces of advice about how to read and interpret a script.

The directors were cool. If I thought a line didn't flow right or read real, they let me change it up. If I said, "This ain't something Snoop would say," they'd say, "Well, how *would* she say it?" I'd say it my way, and my way almost always won out.

There's a character on *The Wire* called Proposition Joe. His real-life name is Robert Chew, and he's also a drama teacher. During the shoots, the producer suggested that some of the younger actors, including me, go to Robert for a few tips. He's a beautiful man who talks about emotions and instincts and relaxing in front of the camera until you're in the moment of the action. He talks about acting with your heart. My heart was open to Robert because I wanted to learn.

My heart was beating fast that day I read the nail gun scene. I didn't get it. I called in Ed Burns, one of the writers, and told him plain, "I got no fuckin' clue what's happening here."

He explained that Snoop had been sent on a job to find the best nail gun out there. "You ever been in a hardware store?" he asked me.

"Sure," I said. "When Pop was alive, I went all the time. Him and me lived in hardware stores."

"Well, that's all it is. You're walking through the door, inspecting all the merchandise. You come up to the clerk and ask his advice. He sells you on the biggest nail gun in the store. You're happy. You buy it for cash and tip him extravagantly. You've scored."

"So it's kinda like I'm going on an errand for Pop," I said.

"Exactly. This is a big scene because the nail gun you buy will board up deserted houses filled with the bodies of people you've killed. It might sound like a routine errand, but it's not. It's sinister, but you play it matter-of-factly."

Next morning I was ready to be sinister. When we rolled, I was feeling it. Everyone said the scene came out good. I don't wanna sound stuck on myself, but I nailed that sucker.

The other truth is when I started appearing on the show, I'd watch myself at home and liked what I saw. Again, I don't mean to be egotistical, but I thought I looked better on TV than in real life. That made me excited. And kept me excited.

I ain't ever seen myself that way before. I had to respect myself 'cause I'd become a professional actor. Being a pro actor made me act differently in my nonacting life.

Before *The Wire*, I was already a little star in the hood. Everyone knew me. But the more I was on *The Wire*, the more it seemed I was a little star all over the country. That amazed me. And it also gave me a different feeling when strangers came up to me and said, "I love your work."

When I dealt dope, no one came up and said, "I love you work." No one looked at me with eyes of appreciation.

"You doing a good job," an older lady told me in a restaurant. "We're proud of you."

Proud of me? Man, that made me feel ten feet tall.

"You're treating this role very responsibly," someone at work said.

Pride, responsibility—man, these were new concepts.

I liked feeling proud. I liked feeling responsible.

I wanted to act responsibly.

The responsible thing was to close down all my shops.

And I did.

Got out of the drug-running business.

Got more and more serious about acting.

Started feeling more positive vibes from David Simon, the guy who created the show and still writes lots of them. Started feeling the love from writers like Ed Burns and the other people who were turning out those great scripts. They was showing Baltimore for how it really is.

I started feeling—period.

Ain't saying I'm the best actor out here. I know I'm not. But I also know that acting, by showing me how to feel, also showed me I hadn't been feeling at all.

You can't sell dope all day and still feel.

You can't kill niggas and still feel.

You just can't.

When I acted out the part of Snoop, I saw that to do the things she does—the murders she commits—she had to shut herself down.

That's an awful thing. That's a fuckin' brutal thing.

Now there's this new thing.

This new Snoop.

I realize the newness is due to good luck or good fate or those good angels who came from Mama's prayers for protection. I realize I'm blessed. Being blessed is a new feeling that takes getting used to.

I'm believing we're all blessed—blessed to be alive. I had that blessing from the beginning but I blocked it. I hid from it. I threw off the blessing. I threw it away chasing some shit I had no business chasing.

The old Snoop messed up that blessing that came from being cared for by good people—Mama, Pop, my godmother. Uncle and Father, though they were caught up in their own bullshit, blessed me by trying to set me straight. They blessed me by loving me. But I flipped off the blessing.

I've come to believe that you gotta believe in the blessing. Ignore it and it ignores you. Embrace it and it powers you.

The old Snoop felt powerful, but it was a power that came from a gun or a bad-ass reputation. The new Snoop feels powerful, but the power is different; it's coming from a spirit I can't explain.

At first, I felt like I had to explain it. Now I don't. I just accept it. I breathe in the spirit just like I breathe in air. I feel the spirit. It keeps me up. It keeps me clear. Keeps me where I wanna be.

I wake up in the morning, yawn, stretch, get up, and look out the window. If the sun is shining, fine. If it ain't, that's fine too.

I'm saying a little two-word prayer. "Thank you."

That's the whole prayer.

I keep saying it during the day. Saying it out loud and saying it to myself.

I say thank you for a new point of view. Say thank you because I'm seeing everything differently.

I'm seeing that the point of this life we've been given is to not shut ourselves down, but open ourselves up.

Open up our hearts. Open up the part of our souls where hope lives. Open up our creativity and open up our minds.

Let light pour in.

Let light grow bright, not dim.

Let love come in and take over.

Let love direct us to where we need to go.

All this is new for me.

All this is amazing for me.

But now that it's happening, now that I've been saved by forces that I still don't really understand, all I can do is look back with sadness and look ahead with hope.

The sadness is for all the people I've fucked up. I'm truly sorry for that. I can't give back lives and I can't undo what I've done, but I can say that I regret it in the worst possible way.

Regret pulls me in one direction; hope pulls me in another.

Hope is for all the good I wanna do.

The people I wanna touch.

The light I wanna give, just as the light has been given to me.

The light has come back, the same light that came down on me in the Cut when I recovered from Uncle's death.

Where does the light come from? And what do you call it?

You can call it God. You call it Jesus. These names are good names.

But I call it the miracle of love.

I call it Grace after Midnight.